Literacy Practices in Sports and Coaching

This book addresses the ways in which literacy skills, including both reading and writing instruction, are introduced, reinforced, reviewed, and refined in a sports or physical education setting.

While there has been significant research that highlights the academic benefits of sports participation and the use of sports programming and units for literacy instruction in the classroom, there is limited research regarding the literacy practices that occur as a direct part of sports participation. This book addresses this crucial gap in the scholarship. The argument presented in this manuscript contends that a number of literacy skills and competencies are taught in and through a number of sports programs and explores how they are effectively and naturally integrated into structured athletics/sports programming. Addressing engagement with literacy skills and competencies in a unique setting, it provides a new lens from which readers can view reading and writing.

This book will be of critical interest to scholars and researchers with interests in literacy education and sports education, as well as instructional coaches, sports coaches, literacy educators, health and physical education teachers, middle and secondary educators, and administrators.

Rebecca G. Harper is an Associate Professor in the Department of Research, Counseling, and Curriculum at Augusta University, USA.

Routledge Research in Literacy Education

This series provides cutting-edge research relating to the teaching and learning of literacy. Volumes provide coverage of a broad range of topics, theories, and issues from around the world, and contribute to developments in the field.

Recent titles in the series include:

Boys, Early Literacy and Children's Rights in a Postcolonial Context
A Case Study from Malta
Charmaine Bonello

Digital Literacies and Interactive Media
A Framework for Multimodal Analysis
Earl Aguilera

Towards a New Pedagogy for Teaching Foreign Language Politeness
Halliday's Model and Approaches to Politeness
Gerrard Mugford

Critical Perspectives on Global Literacies
Bridging Research and Practice
Edited by Shea N. Kerkhoff and Hiller A. Spires

Teaching with Dystopian Text
Exploring Orwellian Spaces for Student Empowerment and Resilience
Michael Arthur Soares

Literacy Practices in Sports and Coaching
Developing Literacy Competencies in Interdisciplinary Environments
Rebecca G. Harper

For a complete list of titles in this series, please visit www.routledge.com/Routledge-Research-in-Literacy-Education/book-series/RRLIT.

Literacy Practices in Sports and Coaching

Developing Literacy Competencies in Interdisciplinary Environments

Rebecca G. Harper

NEW YORK AND LONDON

First published 2024
by Routledge
605 Third Avenue, New York, NY 10158

and by Routledge
4 Park Square, Milton Park, Abingdon, Oxon, OX14 4RN

Routledge is an imprint of the Taylor & Francis Group, an informa business

© 2024 Rebecca G. Harper

The right of Rebecca G. Harper to be identified as author of this work has been asserted in accordance with sections 77 and 78 of the Copyright, Designs and Patents Act 1988.

All rights reserved. No part of this book may be reprinted or reproduced or utilised in any form or by any electronic, mechanical, or other means, now known or hereafter invented, including photocopying and recording, or in any information storage or retrieval system, without permission in writing from the publishers.

Trademark notice: Product or corporate names may be trademarks or registered trademarks, and are used only for identification and explanation without intent to infringe.

ISBN: 978-1-032-49905-5 (hbk)
ISBN: 978-1-032-50273-1 (pbk)
ISBN: 978-1-003-39769-4 (ebk)

DOI: 10.4324/9781003397694

Typeset in Times New Roman
by Apex CoVantage. LLC

For Coach Mark Holliday

Thanks for being an inspiration to your players, students, and even the non-athletes like me. You have made a difference in my life.

Contents

	Acknowledgments	*viii*
1	Pre-Game	1
1a	The Starting Lineup	12
2	First Quarter: Structure, Skills, and Success	15
3	Second Quarter: Cross Training: Academic Skills in Athletics	38
4	Third Quarter: Words Matter	51
5	Fourth Quarter: No Fumbles on Feedback	71
6	Overtime: Relationships Matter	83
7	Next Season: What Can We Learn From Coaches?	92
	References	*102*
	Index	*105*

Acknowledgments

This book would never have been possible had I not met a group of coaches in rural Georgia who were patient and accommodating with this literacy professor who had a lot of sports questions. And I mean A LOT. Thank you to every coach in this study who graciously gave of their time for interviews and questions. They opened their practices, pools, courts, and fields for me and were beyond patient when I asked questions about terminology, positions, and plays. Because of this work, I have met some incredibly dedicated and talented coaches who are putting a tremendous amount of work into their programs and players. Each of the coaches in this study deserves appreciation and admiration for their commitment to the youth in their communities.

Of course, I am grateful to all those who were part of this book, but there are a few who need a special shout-out, as they were constantly on deck if I had a question or needed additional information.

Coach Wayne: Thank you for opening your practices and office for a professor you'd never met before. I have never felt so welcomed by a complete stranger than when I came to your practice and class for the first time. Thank you for your hospitality, patience, and your willingness to be part of this project. You are building something special with your program not just because you know so much about the game, but because you recognize how important your players and coaches are.

Coach Elliott: I hope you see now that literacy is everywhere! Thank you for answering my texts, drawing out diagrams, and taking my phone calls when I had questions (and there were a lot) about football. Most of all, thank you for being my friend.

Coach Ty: Thank you for always being willing to talk with me about coaching and literacy whenever I was on campus conducting professional learning. I can't thank you enough for getting me connected with other coaches so that I could complete this book. Your genuine interest in this work and your checks-ins have meant a lot to me. And of course, thanks for helping me set my Fantasy lineup!

Coach Dean: Thank you for showing up for those literacy professional development sessions, making me laugh, and for not laughing at my lack of football knowledge when I asked stupid questions. I hope retirement is treating you well, but after almost 40 years of coaching, I'll bet my lipstick that you'll be on a sideline "volunteering" pretty soon.

1 Pre-Game

100% Good Vibes. Good vibes recruits talent. Lotta talent wins games.
—*Coach Gary*

As a literacy educator, I view the world through a literacy lens, always searching for examples of authentic reading and writing in the real world, and in fact, it is not difficult to find everyday people doing extraordinary literacy tasks. And while I continue on the daily to look for the ways in which people use words, language, and writing to function and live, for the past year, I have been intently focused on the literacy of sports, though my interest began almost a decade ago.

Now, I should preface this by saying that I am not an athlete, nor did I play sports in high school or *ever* for that matter. However, I am the parent of competitive swimmers, and for over a decade, I have logged countless hours by the pool watching my daughters and son take part in a rigorous swimming program. In fact, I am writing this manuscript from the bleachers at a swim meet! Through these observational experiences, along with my work in schools with teachers from different disciplines, and time spent as a middle grades teacher, questions about the literacy connections in the world of athletics began to emerge.

While I see plenty of athletes texting, sending snapchats, completing goal sheets, and reading social media posts, those are not the literacy engagements that I am referring to, though those are valid and important as well. They are yet another example of the types of reading and writing individuals do to live and function in the world, all of which help individuals practice, refine, and hone the literacy skills needed in a variety of settings. Instead, I am focusing on the specific and deliberate integration of academic literacy skills that are part of their training on and off the court, field, course, and pool. In many instances, athletes are using sophisticated literacy skills as they evaluate plays, break down films, and plan their seasons. They closely read texts, make inferences about players, read texts for specific purposes, and utilize textual evidence to support their assertions. Yet, are the athletes, and the coaches, for that matter, aware of just how often they are implementing and reinforcing literacy skills? I was not quite sure, which led me to begin a focused and deliberate inquiry into the literacy instruction that occurs within athletics.

Of course, student participation in extracurricular activities, including sports, is wide-spread and has a number of notable benefits, many of which go beyond physical and health benefits and carry over into the social and academic lives of youth. According to the Centers for Disease Control and Prevention's 1991–2019 High School Youth Risk Behavior Study, about 57% of all high school students played one school or community sport in a given year, with football being the most popular sport for males, and track and field being the most popular sport for females. The benefits of physical activity on academic achievement have been well documented and studied (Burns et al., 2018; Donnelly et al., 2016; Hillman et al., 2017), and school-based physical activity programs have correlated with better on-task classroom behavior (Burns et al., 2016). Sports participation offers individuals opportunities for after-school physical activity along with social support from coaches and peers, task-specific self-efficacy, and personal enjoyment (Clark et al., 2015; Te Velde et al., 2018). This is especially important because, according to the Shape of the Nation Report (2016), many schools are reducing the amount of time allotted for physical education, with only Oregon and the District of Columbia meeting the national recommendation for weekly time in physical education. In many instances, extracurricular sports fill the void by providing students with structured physical activity.

While much has been studied about the effects of sports on academic achievement (Burns et al., 2018; Donnelly et al., 2016; Hillman et al., 2017), social and cognitive development (Blomfield & Barber, 2011; Bowker et al., 2003; Clark et al., 2015; Eime et al., 2013; Fredricks & Eccles, 2006; Kort-Butler, 2012; Kort-Butler & Hagewen, 2011; Taylor & Turek, 2010; Zwinkels et al., 2018), and collaboration and team building (Eime et al., 2013; Whitley et al., 2018), little has been written that addresses the connections between literacy and the tasks and activities that athletes take part in that are part of their respective sports. Knowing that before we read the **word**, we read the **world** (Freire, 2000; Freire & Macedo, 1987), I began to wonder what kinds of reading were occurring in athletics programs, as those are the worlds so many of our students live in. While there are certainly some easily identified reading and writing engagements that occur in sports such as the reading of rule books, drafting training regimes, and recording workout schedules, what was intriguing to me were the countless examples of sophisticated literacy skills that were integrated by coaches into practice, training, and performance. Considering the fact that a significant portion of the reading we do involves a variety of text types that vary in complexity and take place in our worlds outside of a classroom, it would certainly stand to reason that the sports arena would be no different. In fact, a quick review of several sports programs reveals a variety of literacy skills that are being addressed on a regular basis, demonstrating that athletics is yet another venue in which real world reading and writing reside.

For example, athletes encounter a variety of text types including film, diagrams, statistics, and images, all of which are used to convey meaning about a particular concept or subject. In fact, coaches often layer texts when explaining a play or rule of a game. Instead of relying on one way to demonstrate meaning, coaches often verbally explain the concept, show images or other media, and include demonstrations. Layering different types of text can help coaches effectively convey a message with specificity and clarity. Yet, in classrooms, sometimes students only receive one version of a message instead of these layered texts all built around the same concept or idea. How could this "layering" of material that occurs in athletics inform instructional methods in content area classrooms, and, furthermore, what types of texts (genre, modality, presentation, etc.) yield the best results in relation to comprehension? What could classroom teachers glean from the instructional practices that occur on the field? And how might these translate into the teaching of academic standards? As I see it, the opportunities for collaboration and discussion are ripe and ready for exploration.

However, the actual engagement in sports activities is only the tip of the iceberg when it comes to the literacy components that are present in athletics. Aside from this, the expanded world of athletics offers additional opportunities and examples of literacy tasks, skills, and behaviors that are naturally positioned within this realm. Sports television programming, sports policies and rules, team drafts, applications and games like Fantasy Football, and other components that fall along the periphery of athletics offer a wealth of instructional potential within the academic setting.

An ESPN Epiphany

My initial interest in the literacy connection with sports began almost a decade ago with the ESPN show, "Pardon the Interruption (PTI)." Not being a sports enthusiast, this is not a show I watch, but my husband does. One evening while he was watching PTI and I was reading, I caught enough of the show to realize that it was a perfect real-world example of the genre of argument. For those of you who have not seen the show, PTI is hosted by two sports reporters who take turns crafting oral arguments based on a list of topics called the "rundown." Each reporter is given about 90 seconds to articulate his argument. Once the bell goes off, his time is up and it is the other reporter's turn. Now, how is this helpful in teaching argument? For starters, it is a tangible example of an argument in the real world, but that is only the beginning. One of the best characteristics of this example has to do with the succinct and abbreviated nature of the argument. In order for the reporters to be successful, they must focus only on the most salient parts of the argument—there simply is no room for fluff and extraneous information. If the reporter fails to use his time appropriately and does not include strong reasons, his argument will not be successful. If he strays off-topic, there is no second chance to amend the argument. Successful PTI arguments are as follows:

- Succinct and to the point
- Include appropriate textual evidence
- Have a well-articulated claim
- Are focused and on-topic

All of these items listed earlier are essential components of both oral and written arguments. Thus, they are the academic demands and components that are primary residents of many English Language Arts (ELA) standard sets, and the hosts on ESPN are executing it! A student's ability to craft and draft an argument that hits those bulleted characteristics can mean the difference between a composition that is a slam dunk, or a missed shot.

As a result of this observation, I began looking into other sports programming and found a variety of sports-related programs that could be used for teaching writing and addressing specific literacy skills. Some examples are included in Table 1.1.

Table 1.1 List of Sports Programming and Connected Literacy Skills

Sports Programming	Literacy Skills
Sports highlight reels	Summary, main idea
Top ten plays	Summary, transition phrases
Pardon the interruption	Argumentative writing, thesis statements
Around the horn	Argumentative writing, textual evidence
Full game recaps	Summary, main idea, plot diagram

While sports programming certainly offers a tangible, real-world example of literacy in the media and in popular culture, what about the complex literacy tasks that athletes complete on a regular basis within the context of sports? How about the literacy skills that coaches are encouraging, fostering, and focusing on when working with their athletes? You see, reading and writing do not exist in silos or vacuums that are exclusive to the academic classrooms. Instead, they permeate every part of human existence—through the words we say and write, the responses we construct, and our observations of the world. Sports are no different. Consider this. In the past month, I have observed the following:

- A karate teacher who demonstrated basic moves to his class and then showed students how to merge basic moves into a fluid motion

- A swim coach who told a swimmer to specifically watch the next race and count the number of breaths taken by the swimmer in lane four
- A basketball coach who explained his team's success on his players' ability to dribble-with dribbling being a foundational skill for successful basketball
- A football coach who asked a player to determine which play a specific player would run based on an analysis of the game film
- A gymnastic coach who has her gymnasts record themselves performing specific skills for analysis

What does any of this have to do with literacy? Everything.

Consider the karate scenario. Taking basic moves and putting them into a fluid motion with an appropriate flow, transition, and connection is a lot like fluency in the literacy classroom. When Sensei showed his students each individual move, separately, his presentation was choppy and fragmented. It is reminiscent of students who word call or break their sentences into individual units or words that are segmented, staccato, and disjointed. Fluent readers look a lot like Sensei when he demonstrated how to merge all those basic moves into one fluid motion as they master skills such as phrasing, inflection, and prosody. In addition, learning how to become fluent and fluid in karate involves the ability to determine which moves work best together. Students have to learn which moves should be linked together based on which parts of the body are involved and what physical movement is occurring. It is not enough to just transition between moves; masters of karate know *which* moves should be linked together based on the physical movement and stance. Similarly, in reading and writing, it is not enough for a writer to simply add a transition word into their writing. They have to incorporate the most appropriate transition so that the goal or purpose of the writing is met. That is why a sequential transition word such as first, second, or last will not work when a writer is transitioning from one topic to another. Instead, different transitions should be employed such as although, however, or correspondingly. In karate, movement that flows is heavily depended on physical proximity and stance. Thus, in karate, students are exposed to fluency, but in a different way.

Now let us move on to that swimmer. In this scenario, the text being examined is the race or the performance. Texts are not simply books or words on the page. They can be film, music, images, spoken language, and more. The swimmer was given specific material to attend to when watching or "reading" the race. She was not supposed to pay attention to the start, the finish, or the turns, but was focused specifically on the breathing details of the race of a *particular* swimmer in a *specific* race. Thus, her purpose for reading was set initially *and* she was focused on one particular aspect. In this example, she is establishing a purpose for reading the text (the race) and was reading for specific information which she would report back to her coach. In literacy classes, we call this a close read because we are reading for specific details and reading deeply. In addition, setting a purpose for reading can help improve student comprehension as they establish their purpose up front.

On to the basketball coach. In this example, the coach explained that his team is successful because they have the foundational skills needed to win games in basketball. Because dribbling is the basis for all movements in basketball, players who do not know how to do this are automatically at a disadvantage. They cannot complete the more complex moves and plays because they are built on foundational knowledge and skills that the players do not have. In many instances, these players who cannot dribble yet are like our students who are not proficient readers or writers yet. It is not that they cannot ever complete the complex tasks; it simply means that, in many instances, they lack the foundational knowledge needed to complete the task. Students who do not understand how to effectively construct a sentence will naturally have a more difficult time forming paragraphs or extended compositions—just like a basketball player who cannot dribble will have a difficult time completing a crossover, lay-up, jump shot, or step back because each of those requires proficiency in the basics: dribbling.

Now to the football coach who asked his player to determine what play the opposing team would run. To do this, the player had to watch game footage and pay specific attention to the offensive players, in particular, the quarterback. After watching several sections of game footage, the player utilized textual evidence (examples of prior plays that had been executed) to make an informed assertion of the team's next likely play. In ELA classes, we call this making an inference, a sophisticated skill that requires readers to take material from the text and "read between the lines" to make inferences about certain parts of the text.

What about the gymnastics coach? When her gymnast is recorded performing a gymnastics task, they watch the recorded film and compare it to the film of an accomplished gymnast who has mastered this skill. In this engagement, they compare and contrast the behaviors, qualities, and techniques of both gymnasts and make adjustments (revisions) to the gymnast's performance. By viewing both texts, the coach and gymnast can talk about what parts of her performance need to be adjusted (revised) and how her performance compares with the other gymnasts (compare and contrast). In addition, there is also a reflective component to the task as the gymnast evaluates, examines, and reflects on her performance.

What does all of this tell us? First of all, it is compelling evidence of the link between literacy and sports. Second, it is yet another reminder of the real-world literacy engagements that many of our students take part in on a daily basis. However, perhaps the most fascinating part is the fact that a group of educators, who on many accounts are not primarily responsible for teaching academic content, are providing daily, authentic opportunities for students to engage in and respond to material using literacy as a vehicle and with much success. These literacy tasks are not only frequent but also natural and effortlessly connected to the tasks at hand. Utilizing a variety of literacy skills to complete discipline-related tasks, like those on the field or court, can help students develop a more comprehensive understanding of concepts and material, in both academic and personal settings.

And while the delivery of the material along with the careful connection of skills needed to complete the task is of significant importance, our student athletes are the ones charged with completing these complex tasks. Take a minute and think about many of the students we teach who also are student athletes. Consider the following questions:

- How many of your students who take part in school-sponsored sports perform better academically during the "on" season?
- How is the relationship between a student and a coach and a student and a teacher different or similar?
- What types of specialized knowledge do athletes have?
- What types of literacy skills do student athletes take part in within their sports programs?
- Are coaches in your school viewed differently than other teachers?
- Are student athletes viewed differently?
- How do your student athletes' classroom performances compare with their athletic performances?

As a former middle grades teacher, some of my student athletes worked incredibly hard on the field but, in many instances, struggled in some of their academic classes. Yet almost all the student athletes I taught excelled in some way on the field or court. Many possessed a tremendous amount of specialized knowledge about their sport and the players associated with it, and almost all of them were extremely motivated to do well on the field or court. Those same students whom many teachers called lazy were the ones running drills in 100-degree heat *before* the school year even began. They were also the ones who stayed after school for practice, attended football camps in the summer, completed grueling weightlifting routines, and took part in fund raising programs to help purchase new uniforms or equipment for the team. *And*, I might add, many of these students helped coach teams at the elementary school or church league and/or stayed after to help their coaches clean up equipment and pack up. *Yet*, many of these students were characterized by teachers as indifferent, apathetic, and unmotivated when it came to their academic subjects. On more than one occasion, I witnessed student athletes give an academic teacher a major attitude and sass but turn into a marshmallow with their coaches, pivoting immediately to a compliant and disciplined individual. I had students who never asked me about their academic performance during the off-season suddenly take interest in their grades and attendance during the on-season.

Those same students were often more than willing to assist me with any questions I had about their given sport; from what constitutes a penalty, to demonstrating a crossover, to providing an overview of the latest up-and-coming NFL wide receiver.

All of these observations led me to have conversations with coaches about their feedback process, their instruction on the field and off, motivation tactics, and the literacy skills that athletes were practicing before, during, and after practice. My guess was that many athletes were unaware that the tasks associated with their sport had anything to do with reading and writing and I had a feeling that many of the coaches were unaware too. In fact, when I asked coaches about their instruction, many of them were surprised that what they were doing, which they considered a natural coaching procedure, had academic underpinnings as well.

While I had been tossing this idea around in my head for quite some time, it all came to a head during the year I spent conducting professional development for a school district in rural Georgia. These professional development sessions were specifically for science, social studies, physical education, and CTAE (Career, Technology, Agriculture, and Engineering) teachers and were highly focused on the integration of reading and writing into their instructional settings. As a result, I focused on literacy and writing strategies that fell within the confines of writing to learn, process information, along with number of academic vocabulary engagements. Although we did address some extended writing tasks, most of them were short bursts of writing that could be dropped into any subject area, as these are the types of writings that most often occur in content area classrooms. While the coaches initially came to these sessions begrudgingly as many did not see the connections to their subject areas, over the year, we developed relationships that allowed me to ask some of the questions that I had been mulling over for quite some time. Early in the fall semester, I started asking a few questions to the coaches in between sessions or after the professional learning ended while many were packing up for their next class:

- When you break down a film from a game, what does that look like?
- How do you give feedback to players?
- How do you know which play to run at what time?
- When you prepare for a game, how often do you research the opposing team's strategies/plays?
- How do your players track their workout plans and regimens?
- In what ways does sports-related vocabulary come into play?
- How do you build foundational knowledge about your sport?
- How do you build background knowledge about your sport?
- How often do you have a player come onto the team who has limited foundational knowledge of the sport?

In my casual conversations with coaches during breaks between sessions, I found that almost all of them were more than willing to share their strategies and delivery techniques. As an outsider, the questions I asked were basic (remember, I am not an athlete), and it was apparent that many of them were surprised that I was interested in their coaching on the field. After all, I was the literacy lady who showed up in 5-inch heels carrying chart paper and markers. I was not a likely candidate for spending time on the field and clearly had limited prior experience with sports. In addition, this experience was confined to what I observed on television and on the sidelines. When I asked them questions about their decisions to run certain plays, their explanations were specific and elaborate, with many times them using paper and pencil to show me exactly what a play "looked" like (See Figure 1.1). They were patient and explained

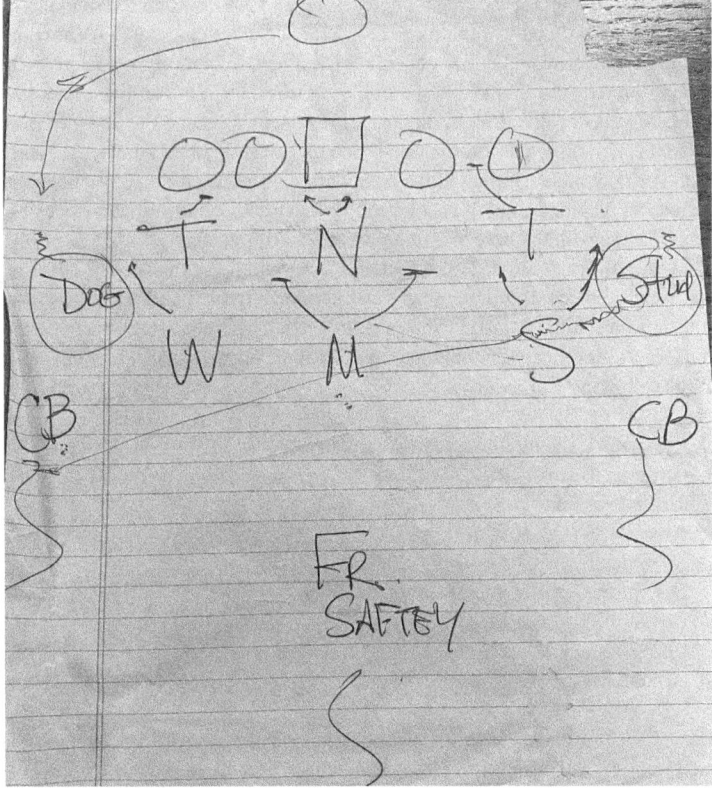

Figure 1.1 Diagram of a Football Play

sports terminology I did not understand, they offered to invite me to observe practice, and sometimes, they even stopped by to see me and tell me something that they thought might be related to literacy after our initial conversations. No question was off limits, and they were beyond gracious with their time and answers, even when I asked questions like, "What does the tight end do again?" and "What do you mean by 'box out'?" Their explanations were often layered, much like their coaching on the field, with them providing me with verbal answers alongside of physical demonstrations and/or written explanations on paper.

Often, I would bring a question that I had to our professional development session for their input. For example, during the fall when I was part of a Fantasy Football league, I asked for assistance understanding the graphs and projections that were part of the app on my phone. I was amazed at the level of complexity and explanation given to me when many of them offered to help me pick my lineup for the week. I quickly began to realize that the statistics on the app were only part of the picture. Instead, coaches elaborated on how one particular player would be a more solid pick if certain other players were in the starting lineup. They looked at the opposing team, location, and who was projected to play for the week. In almost all instances, I listened with amazement as each coach provided information based on research, prior knowledge, and a sophisticated understanding of the content they were discussing. I realized that each sport included a set of specialized skills and knowledge that coaches and players were collaboratively taking part in on a routine basis.

With all this in mind, I started thinking about all the nuances of coaching that were connected to literacy and instruction. What I found during my time with coaches offered insight into a number of basic coaching practices that could have significant instructional implications. In particular, I saw examples of the following:

- Feedback utilizing multiple modes and methods
- Close reads
- Textual evidence
- Research
- Inference
- Discipline-specific vocabulary
- Revision
- Comparison and contrast
- Argument

These concepts listed earlier are all ones that get significant airtime in the classroom and can be difficult for some students to execute in the academic classroom. In fact, these tasks are so complex that many students find them difficult to master and they can be daunting to teach as well. Yet, players and coaches were doing this daily, in a seamless and almost effortless fashion and no one seemed to know that it was even occurring. As a result, I traded my stilettos in for sneakers and began actively seeking out the stories that would explain the literacy I knew existed on the field. What I found was not only what I suspected, but more, as time and time again, coaches and players offered tangible examples of reading and writing practices that were present both on and off the field, offering much to be learned about the literacy practices that are present in athletics and the potential for transfer to the academic classroom. In addition, their communication methods, strategies for feedback, and the relationships they cultivated with their athletes all were pivotal components of their coaching practices.

In the next section, you will meet the starting lineup of the participants in this study. All are current coaches, but in different sports and with varying experience levels. The remainder of this text is divided into six main sections: First Quarter, Second Quarter, Third Quarter, Fourth Quarter, Overtime, and Next Season. Each addresses a specific theme that emerged from the research study, with the last one focusing on ways in which what was learned in this study might be transferred into the academic classroom. Let the games begin.

1a The Starting Lineup

The participants detailed in the following were more than gracious with their time and expertise during this research study. Without their cooperation, this book would have not been possible. While their coaching descriptions and current roles listed in the following have not been altered, pseudonyms have been utilized for anonymity.

Coach Aaron (African American male) is entering his 4th year of coaching. Currently, he serves as the head boys' basketball coach and athletic director for a private school in suburban South Carolina.

Coach Alan (White male) is entering his 17th year of coaching swimming. He is the current head coach for a private USA Swimming team in north Georgia.

Coach Alex (White male) is entering his 16th year of coaching. He is the current head senior coach for a private USA Swimming team in northeast Georgia. He has also coached at the collegiate level and has served as a head coach and program director of a USA Swimming club.

Coach Cathy (African American female) is entering her 22nd year of coaching. While her coaching focus has primarily been on basketball, she has also coached soccer, tennis, and volleyball, in addition to coaching women's basketball at the collegiate level. She is the current head girls' basketball coach at a AAA high school in rural Georgia.

Coach Cedric (African American male) is entering his 15th year of coaching. Currently, he is the head boys' basketball coach at an AA high school in the CSRA of Georgia.

Coach Dan (White male) is entering his 37th year of coaching. He is currently the head coach for a private USA Swimming team in central Iowa. He has served as Program Director for a USA Swimming club, collegiate coach, and age group swim coach.

Coach Dean (White male) is entering his 39th year of coaching. Currently, he is the offensive coordinator for the football team at a AAA high school in rural Georgia.

Coach Elliott (White male) is entering his 27th year of coaching. Currently, he is an assistant swim coach for a USA Swimming club in the CSRA of Georgia. His main coaching experience is in softball and football at the high school level.

Coach Gary (White male) is entering his 22nd year of coaching swimming. He is the current head coach and program director of a private USA Swimming team in the CSRA region of Georgia. He has also served as an assistant swim coach and head age group coach.

Coach Hugh (White male) is entering his 20th year of coaching. Currently, he is the assistant head coach and defensive line coach at a rural South Carolina AA high school. He has also coached softball and junior varsity girls' basketball at the high school level.

Coach Jason (African American male) is entering his 33rd year of coaching. He is the founder of a private sports organization in Georgia that provides sports programming in basketball, soccer, and aquatics. Currently, he is the head coach of a USA Swimming team in north Georgia. He has also coached basketball and soccer and has coaching experience at the collegiate level.

Coach Leon (White male) is entering his 18th year of coaching. Currently, he is the quarterback coach for the football team at a AAA high school in rural Georgia. He has previously coached baseball and golf at the high school level.

Coach Max (White male) is entering his 22nd year of coaching. Currently, he is the head baseball coach and the running back coach at a AAA high school in rural Georgia.

Coach Nate (White male) is entering his sixth year of coaching. Currently, he is the Junior Director for a private USA Swimming team in the CSRA of Georgia. In addition to serving as a swim coach, he has also served as a strength and conditioning coach for a variety of sports.

Coach Neal (White male) is entering his 12th year of coaching. Currently, he is the defensive coordinator at a rural South Carolina AA high school. He has also coached baseball at the high school level.

Coach Rex (African American male) is entering his 25th year of coaching. He is the head swimming coach for a city-sponsored team in north Georgia.

Coach Todd (African American male) is entering his 17th year of coaching. Currently, he is the defensive backs coach at a suburban AA high school in Georgia. He has also coached football, wrestling, and track at the high school level.

Coach Ty (African American male) is entering his 18th year of coaching. Currently, he is the assistant coach for the boys' basketball team at an AAA high school in rural Georgia. He has coached basketball and football at the high school and middle school levels.

Coach Wayne (White male) is entering his 19th year of coaching. While his coaching expertise has primarily been in football, he has also coached girls' basketball and track. He is the current head football coach at an AA high school in rural South Carolina.

Coach Wes (African American male) is entering his 23rd year of coaching. He is the current head defensive coach at an AAA high school in rural Georgia. He has coached basketball, football, and track at the high school level.

2 First Quarter
Structure, Skills, and Success

> *Basic skills have to be repped out. That way you don't have to think about it-it just comes natural. Then when you have to make adjustments, it's easier.*
> —*Coach Elliott*

To ensure success on the field, on the court, and in the pool, coaches employed specific instructional approaches during their practice and training sessions. While each coach had specific fundamental skills that were part of practice, they all emphasized the importance of having a consistent practice structure and schedule, along with extensive modeling and demonstration. Because athletes might come into a sport with varying competencies and proficiencies, coaches needed to create opportunities in their practice and training sessions that could accommodate for these differences. In addition, coaches were aware that not all players acquired new skills in the same manner, so they made certain that practices included multiple modalities for learning to better meet the needs of their players. While coaches were building well-trained and conditioned athletes, much of what they emphasized on the field, on the court, and in the pool transferred into the academic classroom, as many of the focus skills were ones that were utilized in the classrooms. Summarizing, reading for a purpose, conducting research, and making inferences were just a few of the academic skills present in the athletic field.

> *If a coach was to not show up for practice, our players know what to do because our practice follows the same structure every day.*
> —*Coach Wayne*

All the coaches in this study shared that their practices had a consistent structure and included certain mainstays regardless of the season or training goals. Because working on the fundamentals or basic skills was such an integral part of practice, Coach Wayne indicated that even when a coach was absent, the players automatically knew what they needed to do because of the established routine. This also was due in part to the consistent structure of practice and training. In addition, coaches indicated that there was very little downtime in practice. Keeping a specific schedule and routine had several benefits, namely, because it aided the athletes in knowing how practice might look daily and what was expected from their coaches. In fact, according to Coach Hugh, coaching practices stayed consistent throughout the entire season. "The good news is like state championship week, it's literally the same as week zero or the first week or the fifth week. If you're playing in the state championship, you've done enough of successful things, player wise, coaching wise, practice wise. So why change it?"

As other coaches explained, Coach Neal shared that his players automatically knew the structure and content of practice, regardless of the day or season. Coach Wayne's assertion that players could run through their practice routines without a coach was confirmed in my observations during spring practice. Many of the football coaches were also responsible for other sports such as golf and baseball. As such, they often had to leave practice early or arrive a little tardy due to the overlapping practice schedules. However, this did not impact practice as the athletes knew the expectations and were on task even when a coach was not present. In addition, because there was more than one coach on staff who was responsible for the sport, when one coach was absent or late, other coaches were on site to fill in.

Like others, Coach Dean shared that practice was structured in a similar manner each week, with specific days or times focused on different items. In some instances, players worked in small groups with their specific coach, while at other times, they worked in larger groups or together as a team. While there were some variations dependent on their upcoming opponent or training focus, the overall structure stayed consistent. He went on to explain that preparation for an upcoming opponent included building on the same practices and plays that the team had been doing prior. According to Coach Dean, about 80–90% of what teams would do the following week is what they always did, with 10–20% being items that were new or involved tweaking or refining their practice. Some of what they trained for was specialized for their upcoming opponent, especially if the upcoming opponent employed unique tactics or plays. This might include a new play, defense, or blitz, but most of it built on what the players already knew and were well versed in. As a general rule, how players prepared during practice for their upcoming games and races had similar components and parts, and this consistency aided coaches and players in their performance.

Coach Dan described swim practice as having a basic structure starting with a warmup which helped get athletes both physically and mentally ready for practice. Unlike the school-based coaches in this study whose athletes all attended the same school, Coach Dan's athletes came from a variety of backgrounds and schools. While the warmup allowed them time to physically acclimate to the actual practice, it also helped them lose their identities as individual high school students who swam on different high school teams and allowed them to come together as a member of this swim team. After warming up, swimmers moved into a short set that emphasized a technique or strategy, then progressed into the main set, and closed with a wrap-up. Coach Alan echoed this sentiment and shared that he did not change up practice drastically unless, "I'm trying to throw them a curveball or wake them up, you know, on certain days when they just seem lethargic." In addition, he went on to explain that, during their initial warmups, his interaction with the swimmers was limited. "I'm not even counting their laps. That's their time to get ready." As practice progressed, Coach Alan increased his interaction with the swimmers by providing feedback and leading them into their main set or focus of the day which included some common components and structure.

Much like Coach Dan and Coach Alan, Coach Rex's practices have some basic overall similar structure, starting with a light warmup and then moving into a set, but he explained that he was reluctant to do the exact same practice every day because he wanted to make sure that he kept his swimmers fresh and entertained, while at the same time, giving them directives so they knew how to complete the sets and drills assigned. This was similar to Coach Jason's sentiments as he explained that his practice structure was dependent on who was in the pool. Because different swimmers had different needs, Coach Jason's practice structure was heavily dependent on the swimmers he was coaching. Offering them some choice is key too as Coach Rex explained that during warmup, he gave his swimmers options on how to complete this portion of the practice. Similarly, Coach Nate explained that his swim practice structure could be broken down into three basic components: a warmup, a main set, and a warm-down. Practice followed this basic structure daily, and coaches were responsible for designing the components of the practice that would best prepare the swimmers and help them meet their goals. As such, swimmers needed to follow and execute the plan outlined by their coaches:

> I think for the most part, most coaches would agree that, you know, you need that warm up first to kind of get the body prepared, not just ready to race, but also ready to move. You know, as an athlete, I think there's always that edge of you're ready to perform and you're ready to go do things. But I think to get to that next level and really be ready to have to, to net positive results from the work, I think you have to get that warm up phase. I think for the most part, most coaches almost every day would say, hey, we got to do at least some sort of warm up, then we can do whatever we need to in the middle and then some sort of warm down at the end. And for me it's really about just making sure that we're taking care of the body. And honestly, when we're working with kids, taking the thought process away from them just being like, hey, you know, every day you have to do some sort of warm

up, we'll take care of everything else, but you have to do a warmup, then we'll plan the workout, and you have to get the work done.

In some instances, athletes might not know what they need to do in order to improve their performance; this is where the coaches come in. As Coach Nate described earlier, designing workouts and training based on season goals was a primary responsibility of the coach. Then it was the swimmer's job to execute the plan. These plans most often incorporated the repetition of specific skills and fundamentals that were implemented throughout the season. As Coach Dan explained, there were always certain items that were considered fundamentals, and these were incorporated into daily practice regardless of the training season. Technique, starts and turns, aerobic fitness, speed, and race strategy were components that Coach Dan made certain his swimmers consistently worked on improving their performance.

According to Coach Gary, practice was structured so that it simulated the flow of a meet, but in a practice setting. While their work periods were extended in practice, the flow was developed to simulate what happens at a meet, with a warmup, race time, and cool down. While competing at a meet would be much more stretched out with swimmers often spending about four hours in one session, this overall rhythm and flow was condensed in a two-hour practice window. Coach Gary explained that, while the swimmers had a lot more time during a meet in between their warmup and races, the flow and structure stayed the same, which he explained helped them prepare for racing. In swimming, the meet functions as the standardized assessment, much like the spring testing does in the academic setting. As such, Coach Gary's practices are structured to prepare athletes for this culminating assessment, but they also focus on the improvement of skills, mental preparation, and conditioning. Workouts and sets were presented in multiple formats; they were often written out on paper or the whiteboard and were also orally presented. In addition, each swim lane had a copy of the workout available in case they needed to clarify something or reference the directions or instructions (See Figure 2.1).

While swim practice might focus on more individual training, team sports like basketball followed a basic schedule and structure that was centered on team and individual training. Coach Aaron starts out practice with a brief warmup where players come in and toss the ball around. During this period, players take the lead from a couple of teammates who give the instructions for the warmup. After an individual warmup, players start working together as a team and focus on fundamentals. Much like all the other coaches in this study, Coach Aaron always had his players working on specific fundamentals associated with their positions and many of the drills the players took part in were based on these skills. Similarly, Coach Cedric starts his basketball practice off with stretching and warmup drills. "My practice is always scripted, you know, we come in, we stretch, we run, do some warmup stuff, passing, ball handling, then we might go over individuals and work on our offense here, and then we

Figure 2.1 Whiteboard of Swim Practice Set

pretty much get out." When describing a typical practice, Coach Ty indicated that they typically all began the same way with some dynamic stretching, warmups, and activities used to make their blood flow and get their heart rates up. This opening part of practice often focused on five or six different drills which were used to build and practice foundational skills necessary for players to improve their games. Because one of the foundational skills of basketball is dribbling, Coach Ty explained that his players frequently started to practice dribbling the ball down the court with one hand and then dribbling back up the court with the opposite. These types of individual fundamental skills were ones that were a major focus early in the season. As the season progressed, Coach Ty explained that, while they always worked on individual skills, they focused more on team items and more on what teams needed to do to win and beat the other teams (See Figure 2.2).

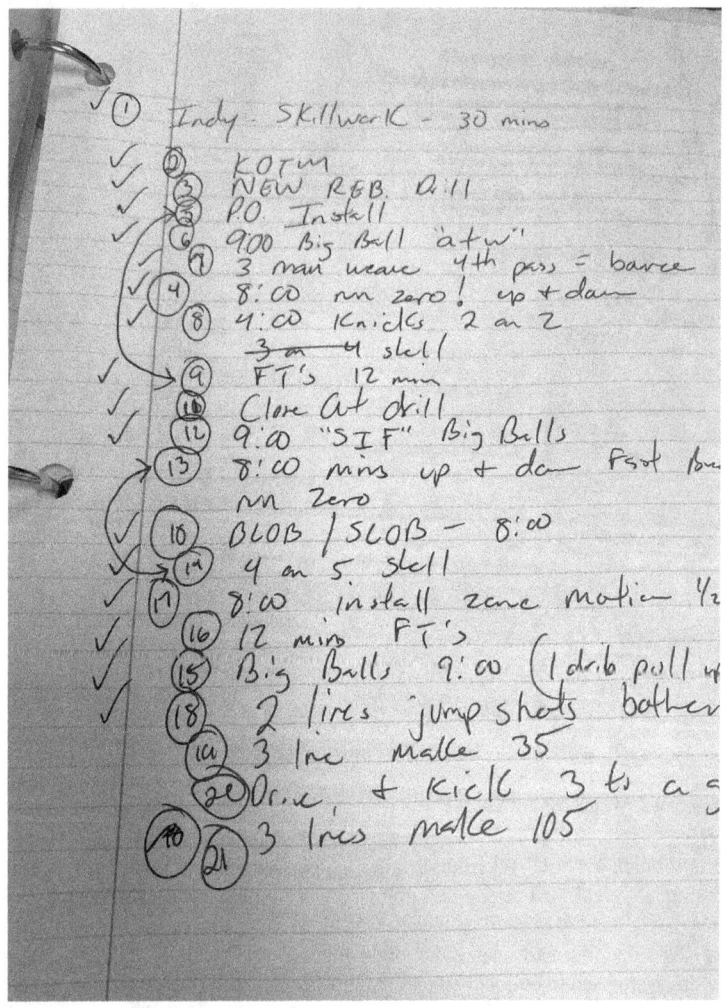

Figure 2.2 Basketball Practice Outline

Coach Todd shared that football practice basically followed the same structure each day with each side of the ball having their own individual time (offense and defense). Each group started out working on fundamentals that were specific to that position or group. After each individual group worked on those position-specific items, typically they all came together and worked as a team, mainly through the form of a scrimmage where players could take all those individual components and techniques and put them together into a practice game. In addition, the week had a natural sequence, with their install occurring at the beginning of the week and practices progressing as the week unfolded. According to Coach Hugh and Coach Neal, on Thursday, their players completed a walk-through of the game plan which they compared with a test review or a dress rehearsal for the game on Friday night.

Like Coach Todd, Coach Elliott explained that his practice schedule had a basic structure, but also included time built in for specific training for different positions:

> Typically, an install is on Monday and Tuesday, and we are pretty much implementing the game plan and what they do and what they focus on, some of the formations we've seen, so we're installing our game plan on Monday and Tuesday. Wednesdays is a team day. It's all the teams including the special teams, defense, offense, all the teams are on Wednesday. Thursday is the walk through, and Friday is the game.

As Coach Elliott described how practice and game preparation were similar each week, Coach Wes echoed this sentiment:

> Normal practice for us is well structured. I would say our practice schedule is basically our lesson plan. Every coach has one. And it is detailed from the time to the period. So, the kids understand at 3:15 we are on the field doing special teams. Special teams are ones that we are doing like kicking, punters, punt returns, kick returns. When that first whistle blows, they know we are going to go into the first part of our practices which is defense. Next whistle blows we are going into offense. Everything we do is a period and there is a time frame. Kids know, and when you get them into a routine, when that whistle blows, it means something.

Setting expectations and having a consistent format and plan for practice were hallmarks in each of the settings studied. Coaches in this study explained they did not just show up for practice and stand on the sidelines barking orders. Instead, practice plans were deliberate and specific and involved a significant time commitment from each of the coaches as each worked to develop and plan practices that would improve their individual athlete and team performance. Practices were often structured into large segments that focused on specific aspects or components. For example, Coach Max shared that his practices were divided into six periods, with a specific focus for each time period. Much like the classroom, coaches mirrored instructional time with their own equivalents to bell ringers, mini-lessons, work periods, closing engagements, and informal and formal assessments. These features helped each coach deliver an effective practice regime that focused on the types of training needed for success. This structured routine helped athletes anticipate the needs and goals of the practice and also helped them prepare for practice. Much like athletics, having an established routine for classroom practices can provide a number of benefits for students. Routines have long been supported from a classroom management perspective (Marzano and Marzano, 2003), but they also can aid in establishing and maintaining a school or classroom culture (Bennett, 2017) and impact motivation and engagement levels (Wright, 2014). Aside from having an established routine for practices, coaches took into account the individual needs and goals of their athletes and team as a whole. Practices often included dedicated time for the development and refinement of individual skills and athletes received individualized instruction on a regular basis in addition to the whole group coaching. Similarly, in a literacy classroom, teachers should consider their individual students when planning instruction and designing assessments. As some students may not know how to address a deficiency, the teacher can use data to determine exactly what skills need to be addressed. Like Coach Nate shared, a large part of a coach's job was determining what an athlete needed for success. Similarly, developing a plan for literacy instruction that addresses not only the overall class goals but also the individual student goals can help improve achievement. Having an established classroom routine and schedule like the ones employed by the coaches in this study can aid students not only in their literacy practice but also in their overall academic performance.

> *We are always going to work on defense. We work on rebounding in some form or capacity every day. You definitely have to shoot every day and work on your offense every day. Those are the basics. Those things are where the game is won or lost-in those basic elements.*
> —Coach Cedric

When examining academic standards and instructional benchmarks in education, it is not unusual to see skills and standards that build on fundamental skills. Before students are expected to master a complex and sophisticated skill, they begin by focusing on the specific components and concepts that connect with the more advanced skills. Unfortunately, in many academic settings, the expectation for mastering these basics might be from a prior grade level or different content classroom, with some teachers not having the luxury of going back to the foundational skills that were not mastered in a prior grade or class. In fact, many academic standards at the middle grades and secondary levels assume that students have at least a base-level mastery before they begin working on a new concept. Without the basics and fundamentals, many students cannot be successful because they lack the foundational skills and knowledge needed to move on to the more advanced topic.

Focusing on the fundamentals of a sport was something that all coaches indicated was a central component of practice. In some instances, this was done in a small group setting depending on the sport, but in other sports, like swimming, athletes worked individually to help refine their technique or stroke. Repetition was listed as a key component for getting athletes to master these basic skills. Regardless of the sport, each coach indicated that repetition was one of the main elements that ensured their players could learn a new skill and retain and refine the fundamentals. In essence, repetition was one of their keys to success.

The amount of preparation (practice, research, conditioning, etc.) for the culminating assessment (game day, meet, race, etc.) was significant as Coach Hugh estimated that his players spent about 50 hours each week for what accounted for about a 12-minute test (the amount of time a player might be on the field). Much like studying for tests and other subjects, coaches compared watching films and preparing for an opponent to hours of studying books. Watching films on Hudl or YouTube was an example of preparation, studying, and research for an assessment that came in the form of a game or race. For example, at the beginning of each new week, players received a game planner from Coach Wayne, which he described as a letter from the coach that provided an overview or summary of the previous week and previewed the upcoming week's practice, opponent, and strategy (See Figure 2.3). While a general overview that is meant for the entire team was always included, segments of the game planner were specific to individual audiences. Certain sections were specific comments to the defense, whereas others were specific to the offense. In addition, a summary of the opposing team's roster or personnel was included with each starting player from the opposing team highlighted and a brief overview of their strengths, weaknesses, and tendencies. These letters or scouting reports were used frequently in team sports, with basketball, baseball, and football using these types of reports most often. Regardless of the sport, scouting reports provided players with an overall summary, another literacy skill, of each of the players and teams. Using game footage and in-person observation, coaches created these reports based on data so that their teams could determine how they might address the next week's opponent. Coach Wayne explained it was like a study guide for the coming week's game, with the test occurring on Friday—the actual game. Using the letter with the personnel stats, players watched the film to identify and observe the qualities listed in the team summary. Because they had read about the opponent's strategy, when they watched the film, they could make inferences as to whether teams would run certain plays due to the actions on the film.

24 *First Quarter*

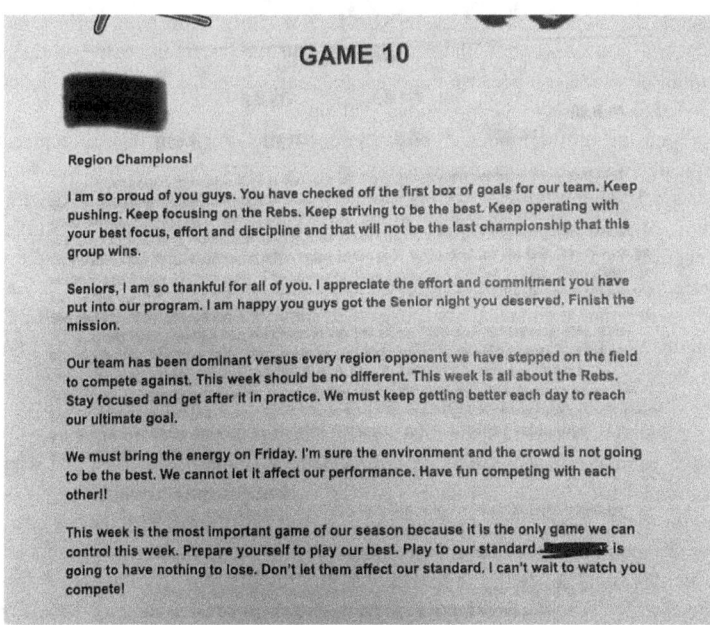

Figure 2.3 Weekly Letter from Head Coach

Aside from scouting reports, preparing for the next week's opponents in football involved using what coaches refer to as a scout team. For the scout team, a group of players runs the other team's offense so that the players will have an opportunity to practice what they might encounter on Friday night. This activity is critical when it comes to preparing for the week's game, or to compare with the classroom, the week's assessment, or test. When players are getting ready to encounter something new on Friday night, coaches work to prepare them throughout the week. This is especially important when the opposing team is running a different offense or uses different plays than the team is used to. According to Coach Wayne:

> When they (the opposing team) are doing something that our kids are not used to or confident in, we have to show them how to do it. So, the scout team is something that prepares us by doing what the other team does.

Using the scout team is another example of the extensive modeling that coaches incorporate in their practice and teaching. In addition, it serves as an opportunity for athletes to take part in hands-on instruction and role-playing which helps them get prepared for their assessment.

The utilization of the scout team was one way that Coach Wayne differentiated between the skill levels of different players. Even if a player was not considered a starter, or a more experienced player, they were still getting "coached up" during practice. When asked what that term meant he explained that even during the scout team when they might be mimicking what the opponent was doing, they were still getting coached on the fundamentals. It might be their stance, their alignment, or their first steps, but even during this period, they were getting feedback and coaching on different aspects of their positions.

Like other sports, scouting reports were sometimes used in basketball, but Coach Ty explained that these were more heavily relied on when they made it to the regional games. During that stage of the season, these scouting reports were highly detailed as the stakes were higher as they moved into the playoffs and championships. And while scouting reports were not used in swimming, there were many occasions when coaches had athletes viewed video footage of certain swimmers or watched their competitors during race day to observe their technique and race execution. In addition, many swimmers had professional or collegiate athletes they followed online, and they used these opportunities to refine their technique but also gain a competitive edge over their opponents in the pool.

Like if you were in a math class and you did multiplication tables with fifth graders every time you walked in there for ten minutes. You know how fast I could tell you 12 times 12 is 144? Because its repetition, repetition, repetition, repetition.

—Coach Max

For sports like swimming, which focused more on the individual's performance, the importance of practicing specific items and maintaining a routine in practice was just as important as that of team sports. While team-centric sports might have entire groups of athletes who practice the same type of fundamentals because of their common positions or roles on the team, swimmers often focused on fundamentals related to specific components of a swim, including starts, turns, and breakouts. In addition, swimmers who specialized in certain strokes or who were distance swimmers or sprinters might have different fundamental basics than their teammates. To train their athletes effectively, coaches needed to know each player's goals, strengths, and weaknesses and build practices and engagements around this knowledge.

Of course, different players in team-centered sports had distinct fundamentals as their training focus. According to Coach Wayne, "Every group has their core values, and they are going to work on those every day." With the goal being to create better football players every day, focusing on fundamentals helps Coach Wayne's players achieve this goal. For example, linemen often worked on blocking their angles, while running backs and quarterbacks worked on aiming. Wide receivers worked on catching the football while defensive backs worked on their footwork and eye discipline. For each of these groups, these repeated activities served as the fundamentals of football for that position. Before players could move on to mastering a more sophisticated skill, they had to be proficient in fundamentals. Coach Wayne explained that taking a player on to a more advanced skill before they mastered the fundamentals was like "setting them up for failure."

This specialized instruction in athletics can be easily connected to the literacy classroom. In classroom literacy instruction, small groups are often used to work on targeted literacy skills that are based on individual instructional needs. Similarly, in a writing workshop setting, you often observe students at different stages in the writing process or focusing on different aspects of the writer's craft. However, there are always basic skills that need to be addressed frequently. As a writing teacher, the skills that I would refer to as fundamentals are sentence construction, organization, knowledge of audience, and a clear articulation of purpose. Regardless of the genre of writing that students complete, the ability to organize it effectively is an important fundamental of writing. As such, these are some of the skills and components that are always at center stage regardless of the genre or topic. These would be the skills that we would make sure to "rep it out," as the coaches stated, for my students to become proficient in these basic skills.

Regardless of the sport, all the coaches in this study explained that foundational skills in their respective sports were the key to their success. In addition, all coaches indicated that their athletes were aware of the purposes of their drills or practices. In many instances, players were given specific items to attend to so that they could transfer this to their performance. Drills were often athlete-specific, thus emphasizing the individualized nature of instruction in the athletic setting.

As stated before, repetition was key for performance, as Coach Cedric explained that his practices always included time to work on defense, rebounding, shooting, and offense. Because these were the items that often dictated whether a team would win or lose, practices always addressed those components. And Coach Cathy explained that, by repeating something over and over, the players got better and could complete the activity faster:

> I think I compare that sometimes to in the classroom. As I get better at doing this problem, then I'm going to do it faster than when I first learned it. I mean, if I'm doing a one-step equation then, boom, I'm done once I get better. So that's why (I say) pace and tempo, pace and tempo and you have to go at game pace. You can't simply stay at what you think is okay; it's not going to be what happens on Friday night. The other team is practicing. It's gonna be at a different pace at a different level. And so pace and tempo means I need y'all to pick it up and get that conditioning in also.

Basketball execution and play were significantly different from that of football because, in a basketball game, a team could quickly shift from being on offense to defense in a matter of seconds. Because basketball is so unique from other sports such as football, where there is a transition time between defense and offense, basketball players must be ready to transition quickly from offense to defense due to the rapid progression of the game. Most of the players on Coach Cathy and Coach Ty's teams held positions in both offense and defense due to the nature of basketball. In football, players often spent more time executing their offense before the game shifted and the ball turned over, but that was not the case on the basketball court. Thus, the transition from offense to defense was an important focus during practice due to the structure of the game. Offensively, players needed to focus on getting the ball down the court in a hurry, while the defense drills focused on trying to stop the opposing team from getting the ball down the court. Coach Ty explained:

> It's not like in football where we have a group that we set for our defense and a group we set for offense. If you have the ball, and I take it from you, I'm on offense now. If I have the ball, you got to guard me; you're on defense now. If I shoot the ball and you get the rebound, you're on offense now.

This feature required coaches to train their players differently than other sports. Since being on defense and offense shifted so rapidly, training only for defense or offense was not congruent with basketball. Instead, he explained that most players would specialize in specific positions, but he clarified that the differing offensive and defensive positions needed to have similar demands or characteristics. "So (in football) your quarterback would not be your offensive lineman, two different skills, two different sizes, two different everything." In basketball, players assumed different positions or roles based on the characteristics and requirements of the different positions. Different players had different specialized skills—some based on their athletic ability and others based on their size and stature. Larger guys who were not as fast and could not handle the ball well played close to the basket because their size and strength helped them utilize these characteristics for their benefit and that of the team. Thus, individual skill sets helped dictate which positions players might occupy.

While much of post-race and post-game coaching focused on preparing for the next meet or opponent or corrections and refinement, coaches described how they were always working on some basic skills regardless of the opponent or phrase in training. Coach Wayne explained that no matter who they played each week, there was always time to work on fundamentals which would help his players improve their skills. In addition, players also took part in what classroom teachers would call small group learning. In this setting, players from different positions would break off into individual and purposeful groups where they would work with a coach on a skill or task that was directly related to their relative position. In some cases, players might not need instruction on a certain skill, and during that time, they worked with a coach on correcting mistakes from the week prior. During special teams time, coaches called different special teams, with one example being the punt team. When the punt team was working on specific strategies and techniques for the upcoming game, those not on that special team focused on correcting mistakes from the prior game.

Coach Cathy explained that even when preparing for next week's game, where practice sessions might focus on game strategy or a specific skill, there was always time during practice to address basic basketball fundamentals. For example, during one practice, players were running down the court practicing a two-ball dribble. While dribbling with two basketballs during a game is not a skill that the athletes would use in game execution, that drill helped athletes improve their balance and train their non-dominant hand. "Whatever they do with their right hand they have to do with their left, so it (this drill) would tell you which hand is weaker until you are able to pound it (the ball) up the same time consistently." While several of the players could not do the double dribble when they first began practice in the beginning of the season, Coach Cathy stated that because they used this drill as a fundamental and repeated practice item, all athletes improved. This strategy helped players during game time because they often had to dribble with their non-dominant hand. Drills like these helped athletes refine their skills and improve from a foundational aspect and were purposeful and intentional as they were used for continued improvement of performance. Coach Cathy alternated between individual instruction and team drills as she explained that, with individual work, they could break down a position and teach athletes how to maneuver each position as an individual.

Like the other coaches in the study, Coach Cathy explained that she did not add new sets to their playbook until her players had mastered others. As such, she did not move on to more advanced sets or different ones until her athletes knew the basic ones learned initially. This allowed them a level of mastery before progression. It also aided the players in building a solid foundation before they moved into more complex and complicated plays or sets.

Foundational skills were also a significant part of Coach Adam's teaching. Much like the other coaches explained, focusing on specific skills that helped his swimmers become better overall athletes was especially important. Some of these foundational skills included (streamlines and breakouts). Many of these foundational skills helped the swimmers as they progressed in their sport as having a solid mastery of the foundations aided them in improving their technique and overall performance. Similarly, Coach Wayne explained that mastering a few plays initially was important, and before they added any others to their playbook, they needed to master those basic ones. "Once the play goes into the book, that's what we are working on. If it's not in our book, then we ain't working on it." While occasionally, Coach Wayne explained that midway through the season they might add a new play in the book if they found that one of their plays was not as productive as anticipated, this was unlikely. However, adding tags or simple variations to these core plays was very common. Coach Max echoed this sentiment by explaining:

> I'm gonna take my six plays and dress them up. We can dress it up with eye candy, tags and tweaks, but I'm gonna come at you with my most basic game plan. It's a very simple, simple plan and when it's simple, all these cats play better. They don't have too much on their plates. When it's simple in the classroom, they do better too.

Mastering the basics and the fundamental components of each sport was an important aspect of athletic coaching. In addition, by emphasizing the basics and individual components that made up more complex skills, coaches ensured that their players would be successful. It did not also matter if a player *should* know how to execute a certain drill or perform a task; if they did not know how to do so, coaches made certain they mastered those items first. In addition, coaches worked to ensure that before any new complex tasks, plays, or drills were implemented, their players were well-versed in those foundational aspects of the game. This philosophy helped them ensure that their players were taught deep and not wide, instead of what traditionally occurs in classrooms where students are taught wide and not deep. Their focus on foundations and repetition helped them train well-developed athletes in a purposeful and strategic manner.

> ***So it's getting ready to play. You're trying to be the best you can be and win as many games and prepare our student athletes the best we can.***
> ———***Coach Leon***

Although athletes were focused on improving their overall performance, getting ready for the next opponent or race day was a crucial part of training and coaching instruction. This was evident across multiple sports as each coach had a plan for their opponents or their upcoming race. Knowing each player's strengths and competencies helped coaches plan their games and strategy. Athletes were sometimes referred to as personnel and teams built their season plan around the players who were on the team. Coach Leon explained that the plays they ran and the strategies they employed heavily depended on their personnel.

> Like this year, we had a 6'5" quarterback that could throw the football pretty well. So we threw it more than in the past. We have receivers who can catch it. We weren't as big upfront as we've been in the past, so we threw it more.

Next year, we don't have that 6'5" quarterback, so I mean, we'll still have our basic stuff right here, but we'll probably do more read option, RPO, you know. Outside, run quick game.

These comments made me think of the academic classrooms where we meet students where they are. In the literacy classroom, we often have students who are not reading on grade level, and in some instances, they are reading significantly below grade level. As a teacher, I cannot present grade-level texts in front of students who are reading well below grade level. Instead, I should present content utilizing a variety of text types on differing reading levels to meet the needs and abilities of my students. Knowing the strengths and abilities of the players on the field helps coaches make the right decisions when it comes to strategy; the same can be true for the academic classroom. While taking individuals with different strengths and getting them to perform together as one cohesive unit was a challenge each week, according to Coach Leon, determining the skill sets of individual athletes helped coaches plan and implement instruction that would capitalize on these skill sets.

This also reminded me of a literacy experience I had a few years ago. Over the course of the past five or six years, I have developed several literacy escape rooms for the classroom. These escape rooms are modeled after popular entertainment venues where the task at hand is to escape from a locked room by solving a variety of clues. With this in mind, I created my own centered around novels, science content, and more. When implementing this in the classroom, one of my first observations centered around the collaborative nature of the task. The groups that were most successful were the ones that identified their "personnel" early on. Like the coaches, the groups that performed this literacy task had to determine what strengths each individual had and then they developed a plan based on their group members. As the escape room task involved a series of puzzles that demanded different skill sets, groups that identified which group members were best suited for each task were the most successful. Groups that did not do this had noticeable difficulty completing the task. Just like coaches, when teachers consider their students and their unique individual strengths and build instructional experiences around these considerations, instruction can be much more successful.

> *We have about six plays that we hang our hats on at a time. For twenty years I've ran six football plays. If I can't get these six plays blocked well and ran well and executed well, or if you can stop them defensively, I'm gonna get my ass beat and it's not gonna be good. So I teach these six plays with a basic formation and then we rep, rep, rep.*
>
> —Coach Max

Preparation for games, though each was strategic based on the opponent and the personnel available, also utilized the element of repetition so that players were prepared to come game night. Sets that were planned for game night were also run in practice so players could get a feel for how the matchup might transpire. Practice and repetition were emphasized by Coach Leon when he reflected on getting his players ready for game day.

> If you look at the Friday schedule, like that's a lot of plays and it's just trying to give them as many reps as possible so that they can it and react to it. And then all of a sudden it becomes easy on Friday night. It's just repetition, repetition, repetition.

Preparing players for Friday nights involved coaches giving them the most accurate and realistic representation of what they would encounter on Friday as possible. One basic item had to do with football placement. As Coach Dean explained, it was important for players to practice running plays with the football placed at different locations on the field because, on Friday night, the ball would rarely land in the dead center of the field. "Every time It's going to be in different places and our guys need to get used to lining up with the ball at different places in the field."

While several of the coaches in this study explained the importance of planning for their opponent and studying the opposition, Coach Ty shared that, first and foremost, they worried about themselves. While preparing for the opponent was important, making sure that his team could do what they were supposed to do was the most important component. "No matter what another team does you're prepared for anything." Like other coaches in this study, examining film of their opponents was a major part of game preparation, and coaches often collaboratively reviewed film. He expressed that there was significant value in meeting with others on the coaching staff after they had reviewed the same film so that they could discuss what each individual had observed. Getting diverse perspectives helped the coaching staff better prepare for the upcoming game. This helped build a strategy for game day as they had to consider what they needed to do to prevent them from scoring, how to stop them from running away with the ball, and so on. Athletes were also part of the game film examination and could often provide another perspective. In some cases, players saw items either on film that were made available online or in QwikCut. QwikCut is a software program utilized by basketball teams and players. For example, players on Coach Cathy's team often conducted their own research outside of practice. In fact, on one occasion when Coach Cathy brought in film of the opposing team on Monday, her players told her they had located film online of the same team and had already watched their opponent. This was not uncommon in team sports as multiple coaches shared that their players often located clips of their opponents on social media or on YouTube. Some of the athletes even attended opponents' games to try and gain an edge on their competitor.

This use of video footage was a hallmark of preparation regardless of the sport. Players examined post-game film from previous games to reflect on their performance and highlight areas for improvement, but they also looked at film for upcoming opponents so that they could determine the strategy and approach for the coming weeks. While sports such as swimming also utilized film, their integration differed from that of a team sport. In swimming, athletes often viewed film to critique their individual technique and performance or used it as an exemplar of what they were trying to attain in practice. This was different from sports such as football or basketball which utilized software programs such as Hudl or QwikCut for sharing film. Hull is a software program utilized by football players and coaches. For team sports, players and coaches utilized film study of their opponents which aided in developing a game day plan. In fact, viewing film was such an integral part of coaching and practice; many coaches in this study shared that by the time their players showed up the next day after the game, most of them had already watched the game film.

While most team coaches explained that they viewed film first as a coaching staff, with defensive football coaches focusing on the offense and offensive football coaches focusing on the defense, all explained how important viewing film was in their coaching. In addition to coaches watching film, so did players. Coach Dean explained that players often watched film of other teams and focused on a specific player to get ideas on how to improve their performance. Other times they watched film of their own games and critiqued their performance.

From a coaching perspective, film became an important lesson-preparation tool for many coaches. Coach Todd emphasized the importance of film work in their game planning and practice. He explained how each week he began his coaching work by breaking down the film into segments which included Coach Todd drawing out individual formations. Using Hudl, coaches can code individual segments of film with specific names and codes so that they can collapse all examples of a particular play or offense by looking for a specific code. Much like qualitative researchers do when they code data such as interview transcripts or documents, coaches are essentially performing the same action utilizing the software. When breaking down the film with the coaching staff and players, they can make inferences about opposing teams based on the film evidence. While Coach Todd called these inferences "tendencies," the action itself is the same as an inference in literature or using other texts. In addition, in many instances, Coach Todd shared that his players often aided coaches in coding the film. This often occurred when they watched game film together and players would share that a particular clip as an example of a tactic or play.

As Coach Leon worked with the quarterbacks only, he had his players watch film after practice on Mondays, Tuesdays, and Wednesdays during the in-season. Film might be from the past week's game where they were addressing areas of strength or areas for improvement, or they might watch their opponent to determine what their tactics might be for the upcoming week. They might pay attention to specific players from the opposing team's defense to counteract what might be coming for them on Friday. While coaches were doing most of the calls from the sideline, as quarterbacks, Coach Leon explained that there were a lot of "reads" built into their plays.

> There might be three different things that happen with one play call. You know whether it's get the ball in the end zone or pull it at the end, squeeze and pitch it. You know, there's a lot of stuff built in where it's just not one thing and the quarterback has to be in charge of that and make that decision.

Watching game film helped players see those "reads" in action and improve their performance.

Like other coaches, Coach Ty explained that preparing for the next week's game involved a lot of preparation and research, much of which involved watching film and, in some cases, physically going to opponent's games. This was one of the benefits of living in a small area as Coach Ty said it was easier for coaches to attend games of their opponents due to proximity. However, physically attending games for scouting purposes depended on the current team schedule. Scouting teams in person often provided coaches and players with additional information that they might not see on film. This was echoed by Coach Elliott, a veteran football, softball, and swimming coach, who explained that when coaching football, going to watch a team play in person often yielded additional information that was not captured on film. This included sideline activity, observing players who got winded easily, or watching players who tended to "tap out" early if they ran too hard or got a hard hit.

Starting on Monday, Coach Leon explained that they completed some weightlifting and other training, but he also shared that they took part in other types of activities that were meant to take care of the whole athlete. This involved feeding them breakfast and making certain they had the nutrition needed to play well on Friday nights. Because some of the players got banged up during the game, they also utilized physical therapy for some of the guys. In-season workouts were about 30 minutes and were completed in the morning during a football or physical education class. Once they were on the field for afternoon practice, they began working on special teams and then they began installing any new plays, strategies, or offensive plays for Friday night.

While practice was structured so that they could continue to build on their fundamentals and refine their technique, athletes were also taking part in a reflective component during practices. Watching film helped them identify the mistakes from the prior week and then begin preparation for the upcoming opponent, which included addressing the prior mistakes. Coach Neal shared a checklist and spreadsheet of paper where he made observations from each play which included all his players along with his assessment of their performance for that week. Players got a copy of this spreadsheet which they referenced as they viewed the film with their teammates and coaches. As the spreadsheet is divided into plays and players, it is easy not only for the athlete to receive individual feedback during this time but also for them to reference the film later to focus only on their own performance (See Figure 2.4). Coach Neal explained that, during these film sessions, they focused on the major plays or on the plays in which they were making the same mistakes.

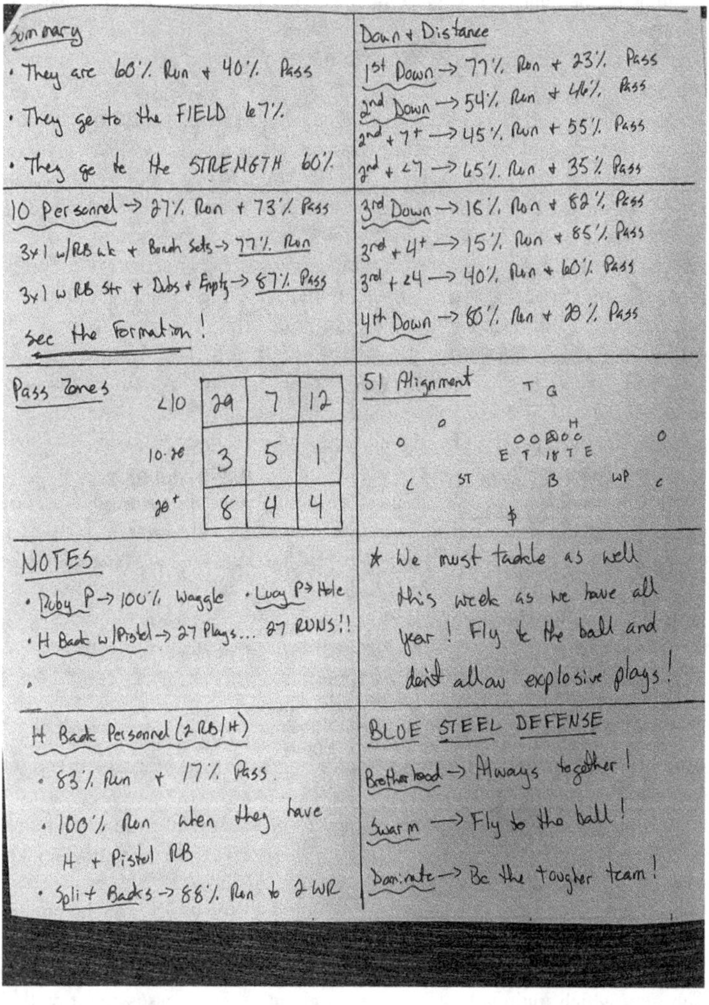

Figure 2.4 Feedback Sheet from Game Film

There simply was not time to go over every single play, but rather, they used their time effectively by focusing on the ones that needed improvement and making those adjustments.

Much like readers do when their comprehension breaks down, players utilize "fix up" strategies to tackle situations on the field. When they realized that a particular play was not working against a specific defense, many times the coaches and players had to regroup and determine where the breakdown in effectiveness or strategy occurred. In some cases, it was in communication, whereas, in others, it might be a player who was not completing the task appropriately. In these cases, coaches ran drills again and offered opportunities for players to respond and correct their mistakes. Viewing film as a team helped players identify these areas in need of improvement and make the needed adjustments. In addition, film gave coaches the ability to provide tangible examples for their athletes. While viewing film offered players the opportunity to address any errors, Coach Wes emphasized how important it was for the team to act as one.

> One thing we try to teach our kids is that if he (the player making the calls) calls it wrong, everybody will be wrong. So if the tight end is on the right and he calls it left, if it is wrong, then everybody is wrong. So that's why we say that if you are missing a call, make sure everyone is going the wrong way together.

Functioning as a cohesive unit and working together to execute a game plan was the ultimate goal, and Coach Wes believed that, even when mistakes were made, it was important for the team to all make those mistakes together. In many instances, coaches emphasized how important modeling actions and behaviors were for success. When working with players in basic corrections from meets and games, many coaches indicated that they would show the athletes the mistake that was made and then the correction that was expected. For example, Coach Wayne described how coaches would use game film to show a specific example and then have the players line up and make the adjustments needed.

Much like their football counterparts, basketball players were able to load and view film in a computer program known as QwikCut. Using this program, players could log in and view film from opposing teams or watch film from their own games. Coaches could track who had viewed film, and this was especially important when players were preparing for an upcoming game. Coach Ty said that he often would ask a player about the upcoming opponent which helped him to determine if the player had prepared by watching the film for the week. These interactions with players did not only happen on the court but also in passing in the hallway. These informal conversations with players aided Coach Ty in continuing instruction and assessment even after the practice was over.

While players watched film as part of their coaching, Coach Todd shared that they had to teach players how to watch film and what to observe. Depending on the position, different players paid attention to different aspects of the film. He explained that he often told players:

> Watch the guy in front of you. You gonna be playing in front of him. See how he moves; see what moves he likes to go to in certain situations. And then that gives you a competitive advantage as an individual ball player.

In doing this, Coach Todd was helping his players establish a purpose for viewing or reading the film. In literacy, we know that when students set a purpose for reading, their comprehension improves (Tovani, 2000). This is partially because setting a purpose for reading frontloads the type of information a reader might look for when they begin reading the text. Much like readers do with books, athletes often exercise this skill in practice and in examining and reflecting on game film or races. While sports differ in their strategies for upcoming games and/or races, each coach described a way in which their athletes set a purpose for reading. In football and basketball, this often was centered around how coaches and players examined and critiqued film. With these sports, coaches interrogated film for a number of purposes. In some cases, they examined film of their last game to determine what plays were effective and what team strategies worked best. This often required players to reflect and critique not only their own performance but also that of their teammates. Once the prior week's game was examined, coaches often moved on to preparing for the next week's opponent. Coach Todd equated the Friday night game to test day. Their performance on Friday was always evaluated, and if a player received the equivalent of a bad grade (poor performance) on Friday night, he explained that it was in their best interest to improve so that they would have a better performance the following Friday.

While that was one way that Coach Todd worked with players on watching film, he explained that sometimes athletes came to the coaches with observations that they made from watching the film and suggested specific strategies that coaches might employ. Knowing how to prepare and respond to a different team that may demand a different type of offense or defense can be compared with the ways in which readers attack or approach different types of texts. The way a reader attacks a narrative is significantly different than the way a reader addresses a non-fiction text. Part of this is connected to the purpose of the text, but also the structure. Narratives are, by nature, structured differently from informational or expository text. As such, the way in which we read and respond is different. Just like Coach Todd's players must make observations of their opponents and then strategically respond, the same is true when reading. What if student-athletes knew that this same type of observational strategy could help them in the academic classroom?

I think sometimes people think we are that lazy guy who hangs out in the gym and rolls the ball out. You know, we just show up to practice and toss the ball around.

—**Coach Leon**

Unlike this quote, coaches in the study did anything but simply show up. Regardless of the sport, each coach shared how their practice plans and components are strategic and purposefully planned. Their consistency and the structured form of practice help contribute to their athletes' quality of training and season goals. In addition, their deliberate focus on the fundamental aspects of their sports helped them train and build athletes who have a solid foundational knowledge of their sport and were well-trained in the basics before moving on to more advanced materials. It is also worth noting that even when athletes mastered a basic skill, coaches continued to practice it even after mastery. Basics were not forgotten, and they certainly were not checked off on a standards matrix. Instead, they were a fundamental component of practice from start to end, regardless of the skill level. These characteristics and practices helped coaches build, sustain, and support strong and successful athletes.

3 Second Quarter

Cross Training: Academic Skills in Athletics

> *Bring your own guts. I can't coach guts. You either got guts or you don't. But if you miss a block, I can teach you how to get that better. If you're not quite fast enough, we can work on that. If you're not quite strong enough, I can help you with that. But I can't teach you guts.*
>
> —Coach Max

All the coaches in this study were not only focusing on a set of basics on a regular basis but also frequently implementing new techniques, drills, or plays. When addressing new skills on the court, field, or in the pool, coaches had to employ effective teaching and instructional strategies for these new skills. While each coach had a tactic and plan for teaching new skills, there were several common components across multiple sports. Teaching a new skill often involved a layered approach to instruction. These layers might include a film or video clip, a demonstration from a coach who modeled the act, and then a player physically performing the action. While a significant amount of reading was taking place, many of the texts used were images, videos, manipulatives, or human models. Rarely did a player read a step-by-step guide on how to block, tackle, or defend. Instead, coaches relied on modeling, showing, and doing. Coach Wayne explained that before his coaches introduced a new play or tag at practice, he preempted the new idea by showing athletes the play that would be the focus. Showing them the finished product or end game first, while explaining why they were learning it and what it should look like, helped players to see not only the *what* but also the *why* and the *how*. Coach Elliott agreed with this sentiment as he believed that there was always a purpose behind a play or a strategy and the players needed to be aware of this during execution.

Teaching new plays often began with players walking out of the play at a slow and deliberate pace. This allowed coaches to show individual players the specific items that each individual player should attend to. Moving at a slow and deliberate pace provided coaches with another opportunity to break down a play into the individual components necessary for proper execution.

DOI: 10.4324/9781003397694-4

Coach Todd shared that his coaches often saw players writing up new plays and models which helped them get a visual for what they would use on the field. Before they ran a new play, coaches diagramed it out on a board for what they called chalk talk. Each new formation or play was broken down and discussed using visual aids and drawings. Players were also involved as Coach Todd shared that, when they displayed a diagram, they often had players come up and draw where they would go in the position they were playing.

> When I call this play, where are we going? Where is everybody going? Not just you, but the whole defense? We have them take the pen and I want to see you write it. I want to see you do it.

Having players write out their movements and explain the plays with written notation was something that Coach Time believed helped his athletes improve their execution.

Like Coach Tim, Coach Elliott explained that coaches did a lot of chalkboard talk which involved the drawing of diagrams so that players could see where they might line up and how they moved. When working with the defensive players, Coach Elliott explained that his players needed to know from the opposition who was their strongest and best guy. Being able to identify this helped the players determine how they might defend that tactic.

Many of the coaches explained that working on new skills or specific components involved a lot of chunking and breaking down of larger concepts into smaller components. When working on starts, Coach Dan said that he would break down the start into each individual component. He would then diagram these components on a whiteboard or paper so that the swimmers could see how that one skill was broken into multiple aspects or components. That way, the swimmers could dissect a skill by paying attention to all the parts that came together to complete the start.

> We might start with a demonstration . . . and then practice it in different steps. We might start just by jumping off the blocks too so their legs will get into the right position beforehand. We'll rehearse the body position, getting the arms out, when to push. And then once we've done all that, we'll put it together, so it's kind of like one step at a time.

While Coach Dan does not always get in the water and demonstrate the swimming, he explained that he often demonstrated on deck with his arm placement or showed them how they might stand or position their feet. Demonstration was a pivotal component of his coaching instruction, and he relied on a variety of instructional engagements when teaching new skills.

Like Coach Dan, Coach Ty explained that it was not always possible for a coach to physically demonstrate a specific skill (some were directly related to their age or ability), but, when possible, coaches tried to physically demonstrate a specific tactic or skill. Coach Dean said that when coaches were "too old and can't run," they relied on other means to teach a skill. Yet Coach Max remarked, "I've always been a guy that if I can't demonstrate it, then damn it, I can't fuss when it ain't right." Sometimes, coaches used another player to demonstrate a specific skill, whereas, on other occasions, they might use video clips or written diagrams. Regardless, Coach Ty explained that it was important for coaches to use multiple methods to reinforce skills since not all players learned the same way.

Much like the other coaches in the study, Coach Cathy explained that, whenever possible, she would jump in and model for her athletes. Her experience as a player helped her with this as well. Sometimes, instead of telling them what to do or having another player demonstrate, she or the other coaches would jump in and demonstrate. "I'll get in there and show them exactly what they can do with the ball." Getting on the court with the players also helped coaches see exactly what was going on and what options there were for strategy and playing. She went on to elaborate that there was more than one way to learn and execute a skill. She wanted her players to understand that there were multiple components that her players had to attend to when completing a skill. Instead of focusing on a scripted way of doing things, she wanted them to modify and respond to their surroundings.

> I compare this to solving equations. Multi-step equations—there is not necessarily one way to do it. I can put a set in and on the court, but if that set breaks down, what are you going to do? Solving a multi-step equation in math class I can do it several different ways and get the same result. I don't have to add and subtract that every time—just do whatever way you're comfortable with.

When learning a new skill or running a new drill, Coach Cathy explained that sometimes her athletes needed additional instruction to effectively accomplish the task. She went on to explain that she worked to build a culture where questions were welcomed and that if they did not understand she wanted them to speak up and share so that they could clarify and correct any misunderstandings. When athletes did not understand a concept or drill, sometimes they worked on it as a whole team while other times some of the coaches might pull an individual or a small group aside to work on the skill. Sometimes, they might pull a player off to the side and have them watch the other players executing the drill that they had trouble with. While watching, a coach would explain what was happening and then have them ask questions. Coach Cathy explained, "Everybody doesn't learn the same. Some learn by doing. Some learn by watching others. So I'll demonstrate it but they might need to see it two or three times." By offering opportunities to learn a skill multiple ways, (doing/seeing/hearing),

Coach Cathy made certain that she was able to reach the maximum number of athletes in her practice.

Much like the classroom, coaches focused on "I do, we do, you do." There was a lot of scaffolding with coaches demonstrating a variety of the activities and then asking players to replicate the action. Both Coach Hugh and Neal explained that demonstration and hands-on instruction were a significant component of their on- and off-field instruction. Coach Neal explained that he often used video to demonstrate a new skill, especially if it was one that he was not athletic enough to complete. Coach Hugh shared that he was probably more hands-on than some other coaches, and this was evident in my observation during practice. "I'm grabbing them by their feet, moving their feet, moving their hands." Coach Hugh was frequently modeling for the players the position they needed to be in or the form they needed to replicate when lifting or executing a drill. Coach Hugh explained that showing students through kinesthetic, visual, and auditory means helped the players retain the information.

Like all the coaches in this study, Coach Gary shared that it was important for his swimmers to fully understand how and why they might run a specific practice or set. While he gave his swimmers short explanations and feedback in many instances, Coach Gary explained that a deep explanation often took place when swimmers were working on a specific skill or technique. For example:

> Like today, I had one where it was about where to place your feet on the block. When doing a relay start, a lot them end up rushing and don't put their toes on the edge and they end up jumping off the flat part of the block. If you put the maximum amount of pressure on it you have to jump up a little and I want them to put their toes to the edge so they can push off the front edge of it, the vertical edge of it, so they can dive out into the water. We talked about three or four minutes, but then I showed them an example. I made one of the boys jump with his feet flat and I made another boy jump with his feet wrapped around the edge to make him feel the difference. I told him to do each one of those and feel the difference. Then I told him to only do the second one (feet on the edge). So that gives them a feel for it then we go back to what we were doing before. If we keep seeing the same mistake, we stop, take the four minutes (to explain), but then we got ten minutes of a much-improved relay start.

When teaching a new drill, Coach Gary explained that they started off by telling the swimmers the name of the drill and then demonstrating it. Sometimes when working with younger swimmers on a new drill, he might have an older swimmer jump in the water and demonstrate it for them. Then, during those times on the wall or during those deeper explanations he described earlier, swimmers would take turns mimicking the drill until they got a good feel for it before they went back to training. "Repetition after repetition after repetition. I try to make those repetitions slightly different every day. It's the same thing though. It's coming in and doing the same thing. I am a big believer in death by 1000 pelts."

Like many of the other coaches, when teaching specific skills and techniques, Coach Alex explained how important it was to break concepts down into smaller more manageable chunks. One example he provided was instruction focused on foot placement and getting power off the blocks. This skill started with focusing on body placement, position, and angles which were all broken down so that swimmers could see how each component helped them achieve the overall goal. He explained that in some cases, they used different athletes to demonstrate different components of a skill. For example, if one athlete has a better foot position or another shows better power off the blocks, they might use both to show each of the components comes together for a powerful start. Peer demonstrations were common in Coach Alex's coaching as he described how this allowed the coaching staff not only to demonstrate the effective technique but also to provide confirmation and praise for those who were doing components correctly. However, Coach Alex also emphasized the importance of repetition when it came to working on skills. Some of Coach Alex's swimmers kept journals to document progress. Though not a requirement, he explained that, for many swimmers, it was helpful for them to see their progress and track their improvement.

Coach Rex explained that, when he first began coaching, he often got in the water and showed his swimmers exactly how to execute a drill or a stroke technique, but after two decades of coaching, he does not do that as much as he used to. Instead, he uses different supplemental texts that include videos of swimmers at different levels and physical demonstrations by other swimmers. He often reaches out to swimmers from collegiate teams who come to practice and demonstrate technique for his athletes. While he considers himself more of a coach for novice swimmers, he acknowledges he is a technical coach from the onset. In addition, he shared that some kids are very gifted and athletic, but for those who are not, technique is an important focus. This coaching philosophy is connected to his personal experiences as his technique assisted him significantly because he was not as athletic as his competitors. Although his focus on technique is beneficial to his swimmers, once his athletes get to a certain point in their training, usually when they turn 13 or 14, he tends to send them to a move aggressive and competitive program that has the coaching resources to train them at this next level.

When implementing new techniques or introducing new skills, coaches in this study all valued the importance of using a multi-modal approach. Instead of relying on one way to demonstrate or implement a new skill, coaches pulled out all the stops and used a number of methods from their bag of tricks. In addition, they frequently repeated their instruction, with players having opportunities to practice new skills on a regular basis which resulted in better overall performance and mastery.

> *I'm a really good teacher because I'm a really good coach.*
> —**Coach Hugh**

While many of the physical skills that athletes acquire in their sports are based on their physical capabilities, dexterity, strength, and agility, others are more academic in nature. Many of the skills that athletes implement in practice and during race and game day are closely connected to the skills that are part of the academic standards and demands in the classroom. In some cases, these skills may be ones that some students struggle with in other settings. For example, in academic classrooms, students are often required to make inferences based on written material or other text types. In my experience working with teachers across the country, many indicate that this specific skill is one that students often find challenging. Yet, many of these same students are making inferences in their nonacademic worlds, including in the athletic setting.

In fact, many of the coaches in this study were providing opportunities for their athletes to make inferences on a regular basis, including as they prepared for their opponent on game night. In football, while there were concepts that teams focused on regardless of the opponent, paying special attention to a specific opposing team's tactics helped teams determine what strategy might be employed on Friday night. Coach Wayne explained that, depending on the opposing team, sometimes his players were able to make inferences based on their prior knowledge and observation:

> When it's easiest is when our opponent's offense or defense looks like ours because now we can use the same language that we use all the time. You know, 'Go line up and dodge right and we are going to do vertical runs,' they know what that means. If it's a week like this when we are playing against a team that runs triple option, that's the opposite spectrum of what we do.

Recognizing the similarities between another team's tendencies and that of their own team helped players infer what their opposing team might do. In this case, background knowledge and prior experience helped players determine what the opposing team might attempt. They knew what types of evidence to look for when determining how an opposing team might execute a play. When teams did not have the same amount of experience with a type of play or defense, making an inference became much more difficult. Coach Wayne shared that, when breaking down film of an opponent, players were asked to supply the evidence that supported their inference. In other words, it was not enough for an athlete to simply tell the coach what they thought a team might attempt; instead, they had to give specific evidence with examples from the film that helped support their inference. In addition, in many instances, they had to watch multiple clips to make a solid determination. By doing this, athletes were acquiring and positioning textual evidence to help them develop and support their inferences. This same practice and skill is scattered throughout English Language Arts (ELA) standard sets.

In the classroom, many times students are asked to apply a sophisticated skill such as inferencing to a text type that they may have limited experience or prior knowledge. This lack of prior knowledge and experience can make this task more difficult as background knowledge is key for comprehension. As Coach Wayne explained about his own players, students in academic classrooms are no different. When they have prior experience with a topic or concept, completing more sophisticated and complex tasks is more manageable.

Yet inferencing was not the only academic skill athletes conducted in their sports. Another academic skill, summarizing, was frequently practiced as well. While summary is an important skill that is used across subject areas and from kindergarten and beyond, some students find summarizing challenging because they are unsure of what they might include. However, all coaches in this study indicated that many of their athletes were composing highlight reels of film that could be used in their college recruitment. Football players often used Hudl to create their highlight reels, while basketball players in this study used a program called QwikCut. When completing these highlight reels, players were able to select clips from games which they could then compile into an overall summary of their performance that could be shared with college coaches. In essence, players were creating visual summaries, sometimes with accompanying audio or text commentary that conveyed an overall explanation or synopsis of their performance.

Like a traditional classroom summary, only the important details were included in this completed product—thus, players found examples of their best performances, examples of their strengths and best assets, and examples of their techniques and achievements for inclusion in their highlight reels. Athletes did not use footage from their worst game or showcase their fumbles or fouls. Why? This is because the purpose of the highlight reel was to showcase and explain their strengths and quality as a player. Essentially, players, as they watched and located appropriate clips for inclusion, were determining which selections best suited their purpose for the task and only utilized clips and components that attributed to this purpose. Whether conscious or not, those athletes who created their own highlight reels were taking part in a sophisticated literacy skill—that of summarization and were utilizing the same academic skills needed to execute a summary in an academic classroom.

Coaches explained that, in many instances, players were creating these highlight reels on their own time with limited assistance from their coaches. While Coach Wayne explained that his coaches showed the players how to make a highlight reel, their instructions were limited, and athletes used the platform on their own. In addition to these highlight reels, athletes often created athletic profiles on websites designed for their respective sports. For example, swimmers could capture all their best times in SwimCloud from meets and upload video footage for college coaches to peruse. They could also track their personal bests over time and compare their rankings to other athletes.

Not only were athletes developing inferences and creating summaries, but they were also conducting close reads when they broke down film each week as they prepared for their opponent. When conducting a close read, readers are completing an in-depth reading of a text, while paying special attention to specific patterns, repetitions, or qualities. For example, in the classroom, a student might conduct a close read on a poem and look for specifics regarding word choice or mood. However, in athletics, when players watch video footage of an opponent, they are utilizing a similar skill set. For example, Coach Cedric explained that, when his players watched film, different players were reading and analyzing the film for different information.

> Like my point guard, he would probably be looking more so at their point guard, noticing and pick up his tendencies. He would probably also be looking at what offense they're trying to set up and what they're trying to run while my bigger guys would be looking at their bigger guys. Like if their bigger guys shoot threes, how well do they rebound? And things of that nature.

Coach Cedric also explained that, when watching their own games as a team following their performance on game night, they focused on addressing mistakes. "We're not looking at highlights. We're looking at mistakes."

Watching film and responding to it with their coaches was the equivalent of studying for a test. Coach Hugh compared this with a test in the classroom:

> So we took the test on Friday (the game) and we're going over it on Monday (the film). We're going to have another test this coming Friday. So now we start learning the new material on Tuesday and Wednesday. We have a review on Thursday and we take the test on Friday (game night).

Coach Wes explained that if players did not examine film, it was like coming to class on test day with no pencil and paper. "You don't know what happened because you did not prepare. If you do not watch film, you are not prepared." While the athletes' preparation might look a little different than that of classroom preparation, many of them were using some of the same skills on the field.

However, literacy skills were not the only academic skills that were reinforced in athletics, but other subjects like math were also incorporated. Like basketball when Coach Cathy used angles for court position, there is a significant amount of math incorporated into swimming as well. For example, Coach Gary calculates each swimmer's base time based on their performance and times in the pool. Swimmers are responsible for knowing their base times and then, based on the color Coach Gary puts on the white board, swimmers calculate their pace. Not only is this an example of another academic skill present in sports, but it is also evidence of individualized instruction. Each swimmer has their own designated baseline; thus, their training speeds are unique based on their ability levels. In addition, their baselines are recalculated throughout the course of the season, so athletes can see their progression as the season progresses. This also helps coaches group swimmers according to their ability levels (stroke proficiency and speed) which aids them in providing the most relevant and purposeful coaching instruction.(see Table 3.1).

Swimmers often conducted their own research online to help improve their performance. This included looking at the Georgia State Swimming website for information, tutorials, or video clips, watching races on YouTube, or researching the top swimmers in a specific event and watching their races to get tips on technique and race preparation. A lot of Coach Dan's swimmers conducted their own research by reading swimming magazines, perusing the USA Swimming and SwimSwam websites, and watching videos that focused on technique. Many swimmers found videos of other athletes, often Olympians or other elite swimmers, which they used as examples of solid technique or skills.

Getting ready for the next game or race often required both coaches and athletes to conduct a significant amount of research. All coaches noted that many of their athletes actively conducted research on other players or on improving performance and stamina. At other times, athletes conducted research on potential university opportunities that might be available for them once they finished high school. For example, Coach Gary explained that his high school swimmers kept a spreadsheet of their best times and the potential schools they might attend (See Figure 3.1). Data from meets were collected on this sheet, and swimmers even recorded the times for current swimmers on the college teams they might

Table 3.1 Practice Key for Swim

Color	Meaning
White	Baseline/speed swimmer can sustain on a regular basis
Pink	Three seconds faster than the baseline
Red	Three seconds faster than pink (almost like a 400-meter pace)
Blue	Three seconds faster than red (swimmers need a one-to-one rest—meaning if their blue time is one minute, they would need a minute to recover—roughly 200-meter pace)
Black	Three seconds faster than blue (All Out)

contact for recruitment. According to Coach Gary, this helped swimmers figure out where they might fit in on certain teams based on their individual times.

While this spreadsheet of data might be overlooked by some as a trivial item, when thinking about the literacy activities that the athletes must conduct to collect this data, the list is extensive. To collect these data, the athletes must:

- Examine each university and determine the division, acceptance rate, and current roster
- Determine a focus for the research-which athletes are they recording times for in relation to their stroke specialty
- Compare data from multiple teams
- Track their growth and performance (data trends)
- Look for trends/similarities across teams

Each of these items listed earlier is a solid academic skill that is the focus of many content classrooms. This, of course, does not take into account other research skills they may employ including source credibility, proper search terms, setting a purpose for research, and more. Because athletes are taking part in research in athletics, it is reasonable to infer that they can transfer these skills into their academic classrooms. In addition, many athletes were using a wide variety of sources for this research including YouTube, social media, sports magazines, ESPN, websites, and more when conducting their research. While it was evident that players were completing a significant number of academic skills on the field, on the court, and in the pool, Coach Leon said he was not certain that all the athletes made those connections, but it was clear they were executing the skill. Similarly, Coach Wes believed, "If you can figure out this stuff right here, then you can understand what is going on in a classroom."

> ***I mean, it's really a year long process for us. In the off season we are working on getting bigger, stronger, and better. During the season we're working on winning games and getting our team cohesive. There's no time off.***
>
> ***—Coach Leon***

School	Conference	Cost	Avg ACT	100 Breast				200 Breast				200 IM			
				3rd best	24th	16th	8th	3rd best	24th	16th	8th	3rd best	24th	16th	8th
University of Georgia	SEC		30	59.6	1.02.37	1.00.87	1.00.96	2.07.92	2.14.68	2.12.43	2.09.92	1.53.76	2.00.41	1.59.74	1.57.51
Georgia Tech	ACC		32	58.95	1.03.36	1.02.13	1.00.15	2.05.89	2.17.27	2.15.17	2.13.83	1.56.22	2.00.94	2.00.64	1.58.89
Alabama	SEC		27	59.6	1.02.37	1.00.87	1.00.96	2.07.92	2.14.68	2.12.43	2.09.92	1.53.76	2.00.41	1.59.74	1.57.51
North Carolina	ACC		30	58.95	1.03.36	1.02.13	1.00.15	2.05.89	2.17.27	2.15.17	2.13.83	1.56.22	2.00.94	2.00.64	1.58.89
LSU	SEC		26	59.6	1.02.37	1.00.87	1.00.96	2.07.92	2.14.68	2.12.43	2.09.92	1.53.76	2.00.41	1.59.74	1.57.51
NC State	ACC		29	58.95	1.03.36	1.02.13	1.00.15	2.05.89	2.17.27	2.15.17	2.13.83	1.56.22	2.00.94	2.00.64	1.58.89
Tennessee	SEC		28	59.6	1.02.37	1.00.87	1.00.96	2.07.92	2.14.68	2.12.43	2.09.92	1.53.76	2.00.41	1.59.74	1.57.51
U of Virginia	ACC		32	58.95	1.03.36	1.02.13	1.00.15	2.05.89	2.17.27	2.15.17	2.13.83	1.56.22	2.00.94	2.00.64	1.58.89
Auburn	SEC		28	59.6	1.02.37	1.00.87	1.00.96	2.07.92	2.14.68	2.12.43	2.09.92	1.53.76	2.00.41	1.59.74	1.57.51
Texas	Big 12		30	1.01.18	1.08.46	1.04.87	1.03.33	2.14.41	NA	2.19.06	2.16.97	2.06.45	2.15.60	2.07.06	2.03.41
Texas A&M	SEC		29	59.6	1.02.37	1.00.87	1.00.96	2.07.92	2.14.68	2.12.43	2.09.92	1.53.76	2.00.41	1.59.74	1.57.51
Indiana U	Big 10		26	58.61	1.01.76	1.01.36	1.00.26	2.07.73	2.14.24	2.13.74	2.08.90	1.55.79	2.00.70	1.56.87	1.57.99
U of Cal Berkeley	Pac 12		31	59.77	1.03.95	1.02.27	1.00.72	2.08.01	2.20.20	2.22.28	2.11.27	1.56.85	2.02.81	2.01.03	1.59.13
U of South Carolina	SEC		28	59.6	1.02.37	1.00.87	1.00.96	2.07.92	2.14.68	2.12.43	2.09.92	1.53.76	2.00.41	1.59.74	1.57.51
U of Florida	SEC		30	59.6	1.02.37	1.00.87	1.00.96	2.07.92	2.14.68	2.12.43	2.09.92	1.53.76	2.00.41	1.59.74	1.57.51
Notre Dame	ACC		34	58.95	1.03.36	1.02.13	1.00.15	2.05.89	2.17.27	2.15.17	2.13.83	1.56.22	2.00.94	2.00.64	1.58.89
U of Missouri	SEC		26	59.6	1.02.37	1.00.87	1.00.96	2.07.92	2.14.68	2.12.43	2.09.92	1.53.76	2.00.41	1.59.74	1.57.51
Virginia Tech	ACC		28	58.95	1.03.36	1.02.13	1.00.15	2.05.89	2.17.27	2.15.17	2.13.83	1.56.22	2.00.94	2.00.64	1.58.89
U of Arizona	Pac 12		25	59.77	1.03.95	1.02.27	1.00.72	2.08.01	2.20.20	2.22.28	2.11.27	1.56.85	2.02.81	2.01.03	1.59.13
Ohio State	Big 10		30	58.61	1.01.76	1.01.36	1.00.26	2.07.73	2.14.24	2.13.74	2.08.90	1.55.79	2.00.70	1.56.87	1.57.99
Pittsburgh	ACC		31	58.95	1.03.36	1.02.13	1.00.15	2.05.89	2.17.27	2.15.17	2.13.83	1.56.22	2.00.94	2.00.64	1.58.89

Figure 3.1 College Swim Spreadsheet

For most athletes who play competitive sports, there is very little time off from training, and that extends to their coaches as well. Although the training varied depending on the focus of the season or time of year, athletes were almost always working on some aspect of their sport.

In general, for football players, off-season time focused more on the physical conditioning of the overall athlete and was less football and team-focused. While larger schools might incorporate football classes as a physical education option, not all schools had that as an option. Spring training focused on the basics of football, and Coach Elliott shared that they did not implement many stunt packages because the athletes might not retain them for fall. They saved those drills and that instruction for the beginning of the official season. Off-season was about getting prepared and planting seeds because, by August, it was too late, according to Coach Tim. This time was when they lost some of their athletes because it was not really the "glamourous part." The price of getting better during the off-season was "mental preparation, running, lifting, and hours of physical preparation."

Coach Leon shared the same explanation regarding the off-season when it comes to football. During offseason times, coaches were concerned with getting their players bigger, faster, and stronger. This meant that training focused more on weightlifting and getting into shape. Coach Dean shared, "We're focusing on getting the players bigger, stronger, and faster during off season, but we also focus on mental training as well."

Earlier in the spring season Coach Leon explained that they would work on certain skills and fundamentals because they had more time and they were not actively preparing for a new opponent each week. This included footwork, throwing mechanics, and working on progressions. Spending time on certain fundamentals aided athletes in improving their individual performance, whereas others, such as progressions, helped them anticipate what a team might do based on their observations. While they always worked on some fundamentals during the in-season practices, this was typically done in a shorter time bracket, say five to ten minutes. Off-season allowed them more time to focus on these fundamentals for an extended period of time.

According to Coach Alex, practice shifted on both the macro and micro levels during the season. At the beginning of the swim season, the focus was on volume, aerobic conditioning, and building a solid base. As the season progressed, swimmers began to focus on making certain they executed the skills properly, focusing on intensity, speed, and other related items. Coach Alex explained that, as his swimmers moved into the state championship meets, the focus shifted.

> We kind of view December as a way to start sharpening up and focusing on power. So starting in mid November or a little bit before maybe, we start focusing in more on quick bursts of speed, max effort for certain lengths

of time and start sharpening up that speed and power leading into our first championship meet of the season. But that also serves as the first recovery phase for the to recover off of what we have done the first half of the season. So when we come back after senior state and we're looking at Christmas training, we can train faster and harder to get more out of ourselves.

Like Coach Alex, Coach Dan described the swim season in terms of cycles. Seasonal plans were based on the end game-end-of-season championship meets, and their macro cycle was based on this. The season was divided into components where the focus shifted based on where they were in the cycle, so, at some points, endurance was the focus, whereas, at others, technique was at the forefront.

Knowing each swimmer's goals and area of focus greatly influenced how Coach Dan provided coaching instruction for different athletes. Because, in swimming, some athletes are considered distance swimmers, while others are considered sprinters, training those swimmers at different paces and rates was a consideration for coaches.

Like if they need to work on endurance, how does endurance for a 50- or 100-meter swimmer compare to a 500 yard swimmer? Finding the commonalities and then just grouping the swimmers together in different lanes, writing a set or work out for the different swimmers in that regard. And like for some of the top swimmers, I'll figure out what they need, like they need to do so many sprint sets, so many distance, like so many fly sets or breaststroke sets. And then that sort of forms the foundation or the basis.

Part of getting better at any sport involved training hard and being uncomfortable. Coach Gary explained that some of his swimmers "struggled to suffer," but, in reality, that is what they needed to do to get better. Suffering during practice helped swimmers mimic what would happen during race day when they would have to go all out, so getting "comfortable with being uncomfortable" was key. Coach Max used a similar view as he explained that, in the off-season, "We get uncomfortable. During off season, we have to grow."

Mental preparation and training were also an important part of seasonal training, according to Coach Gary. A significant aspect of his coaching involved putting some of the responsibility on the swimmers' shoulders.

I use the analogy that I am the GPS unit. I am not driving. They are driving. And they are doing the whole thing since it is their sport, career, their time, their entries, their meets. They just need me to guide them. Telling them which road to go on and which path to take. And if they take the wrong turn, we will rest. It might take a little longer, but we will get there.

Self-motivation, according to Coach Gary, certainly helped with an athlete's success.

> I don't know if you remember the guy from 2008, Jason Lezak, who did the relay. He was about 21 years old and he came in on his own for about 9 years. No one was his coach. He trained on his own. He knew what he needed to do and he got it done. . . . Those guys are motivated beyond some coach telling them to get into the water. They get into the water because they know that's what they need. So I try to; I know I can't force it. I have made that mistake a million times. I know I can't force them to want to be there.

As Coach Gary explained regarding self-motivation and determination, Coach Wes shared:

> I take an approach like this. It is an old saying from playing cards with my mom. It's like playing Spades. I can show you my hand, but it doesn't mean you can play it for me. You've got to know how to play and you have to play it.

Being motivated for learning and improvement, along with a solid understanding of what training was needed for performance, aided players in reaching their full potential. While some coaches in this study believed that this was mainly because the athletes wanted to play their respective sports, others also chalked it up to how coaching was executed, the frequency of feedback, and the relationships coaches had with players.

4 Third Quarter
Words Matter

> *There's a whole new language here. There is a whole new syntax here. We use code words and cheats. It's going to take time. Nothing is going to happen overnight because they have to learn a whole new language here.*
>
> —*Coach Gary*

One key component of literacy instruction is word study and vocabulary. Specific disciplines and subjects employ a specific set of words that are needed in order for students to effectively communicate and explain the key concepts in that field. Vocabulary instruction in the classroom often takes on a specific structure, and in many instances, the strategies used are focused more on exposure to the word and the definition. This is often achieved through more-knowledge-based engagements: words and definitions, sentence construction using specific words from the discipline, vocabulary tests, and other forms of word study and practice. Some may be surprised to know that vocabulary instruction and integration have a natural home in the practices of athletics coaches. In this study, coaches were integrating their own sports-specific vocabulary into their coaching practices with much success. In fact, strategies for vocabulary instruction were used on a frequent basis by the coaches and it was not exclusive to one specific sport. While vocabulary instruction was common in athletic settings, the way in which words were introduced, taught, and reinforced differed from that of the traditional classroom setting.

> *We say, 'Here is the word and here is how to use the word, and not only here is how to do it, but here are some offshoots to it.' If we slant right, it's not just the word 'slant' but how we do it and why.*
>
> —*Coach Elliott*

Regardless of the sport, coaches explained how important it was for the athletes to understand, utilize, and communicate using the vocabulary and terminology of the sport. While each indicated that some words were exclusive to specific teams or coaches, there was a specific set of words that athletes were expected to have in their lexicon regardless of the team association. Many of these were core words that served as the baseline vocabulary for their respective sports. These words were used on a regular basis and introduced, reinforced, and utilized in multiple contexts and were a crucial component of their respective sports worlds. For example, in football, the term "triple option" was universal and was understood by players on multiple teams because it was a phrase used throughout the sport. Triple option is an offensive play where the offense has three options for a running play. Ultimately, three different players had the option of running the ball. However, the term "brickyard" was a team-specific locution that had different meanings in different settings. For one team, "brickyard" was a specific play they used against a certain opponent, whereas 50 miles up the road, the same term referred to the period of practice that was meant to replicate a game on Friday night. Knowing the specific context of words was key for comprehension and was crucial when it came to executing specific plays, implementing certain techniques, or following directions.

This utilization of a variety of sports terminology was apparent when observing practice and interviewing the coaches about their athletes. While some of the terms, like triple option, were more universal across the individual sport, each team had unique terms and words that were exclusive to their context. Although coaches across the country might use different terms for the same action or stance, Coach Wayne explained that his team of coaches made sure to use the same terms across the board for their entire coaching staff. For example:

> For a defensive end that does not get blocked, he's going to get squeezed down to the ball. That's where the language becomes different. Some coaches might say, "squeeze" and another might say "stiff down," another coach might say, "close" and another coach might say, "shuffle." It's the same thing, but to a sixteen-year-old, they might not know what that means and that's why we try to use a common language. So our defensive lineman coaches will teach them "squeeze" and he will hear it all the time so he can know what it means. Each position will have language like that.

Having consistency in the language used for a coaching staff and a team was key for comprehension. This was especially important as many times, coaches transferred to new teams where terms were different. As the Head Coach, Coach Wayne made certain that his team of coaches used the same terms and language throughout so that players could better understand exactly what they were expected to execute. Much like Coach Wayne explained, during interviews, Coach Todd utilized a variety of football terminology including blitz packaging, A, B, C, etc., gaps, coverage, and a variety of number combinations (3/4 defense). For his players to execute any drills or specifics, they had to have a strong command of the language of football. "We have our own language. It's a whole different language out here." Like many of the other coaches, Coach Todd emphasized the importance of discussing drills, plays, and on-the-field expectations using a common language, but more than anything, the players had to know what action each word represented. In addition, using a common language allowed coaches to provide directives to multiple players who played a number of different positions. Unlike college and professional team sports, high school athletes often played multiple positions and were not committed exclusively to playing in one specific position, so common language was a functional necessity.

It was important for the players to know the action that was connected to that word, so, while a player might go 20 minutes up the road and see that another team uses a different term, the action is the same. Similarly, in literacy classes, students often encounter words that represent the same concept but look different. When thinking about words, meanings, and concepts, it is easy to connect this to the academic classroom. Often, students understand a concept, process, or action, but sometimes get confused when a different word is used. In many cases, students might only assign one word to a concept or definition. As an ELA teacher, I saw this happen in the classroom frequently. Think about these words:

- Passage
- Text
- Excerpt
- Selection
- Paragraph

Each of those words has the same meaning in the context of the sentence, "Read the (fill in the blank with one of those words above) below." However, if a student does not know that the word *text* can also mean the following paragraph, many of them may be envisioning something like this:

U see her 2day? WTH?

You see, for today's young adolescents, the word text may mean something different than what it means for a literacy instructor. For students who equate a text to the example above, can you image the confusion when they see a paragraph or a poem? They were expecting a text message but were presented with a significantly more involved written composition. Opportunities to engage not only with terminology and specific words but also with the action or concept associated with them are a crucial component for understanding.

In many instances, this absence of a common language can be confusing for students. As a teacher educator and literacy professor, I often suggest that teachers post AKA Charts or Also Known As Charts (Harper, 2017) in their classrooms (See Figure 4.1). Because we know that many concepts can be described using different terminology, providing students with a reminder or display of these words can aid in their learning.

All coaches in this study acknowledged the importance of utilizing a common language with their players. As Coach Wayne explained, athletes needed the consistency and uniformity of a common language and way of expression. Because so much of their performance was based on communication, comprehension, and execution, utilizing words and phrases that were consistently used across all positions and with all coaching staff helped their players acquire, understand, and utilize the discipline-specific vocabulary of their respective sports.

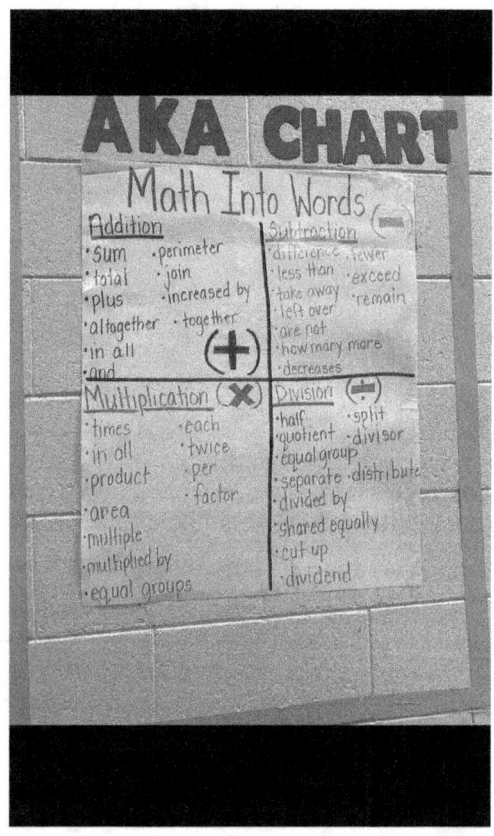

Figure 4.1 AKA Chart

While different teams or coaches may call different drills different words, the language of swimming is similar, according to Coach Rex.

> In all the swimming worlds, we talk about high elbows and things like that, you know, but when we're doing drill sets, the language does vary from team to team. You know, some people say, 'Yeah, we're gonna do the Texas flip turn or the Georgia dive, or something like that.

Much like other coaches in this study explained, Coach Rex concurred that, while the word or term for an action or drill may vary from team to team, they were talking about the same action.

With the universal swim language described by Coach Rex, he explained that it was important to get athletes from a very early age to understand specific words and drills. Although athletes often change teams throughout their sports career, once the kids see an illustration or the drill in action, they can connect it even if one coach calls it one word, while another calls it something else. Coach Rex emphasized the importance of swimmers actually seeing the activity or skill for them to understand and execute it.

Like the other coaches in the study, Coach Alex shared a wide variety of sports-related vocabulary that his swimmers were expected to know. Teaching these vocabulary terms was most often done through physical demonstration with coaches showing swimmers exactly how to perform the action that was associated with the term. Yet Coach Alex explained that demonstration was not all that was done when teaching vocabulary. In fact, he shared that giving athletes the reasons "why" they were expected to perform these actions a certain way was important. "Showing them why you're doing this a certain way, and in turn, that defines the word or the term you are using like streamline. You have a narrow, narrow cross section which means less water resistance." Coach Alex's inclusion of the *why* in his vocabulary instruction was important to note as well. As he saw it, when athletes understood the action along with the why, they had a better and more complete understanding of the entire concept.

In addition, many of the football coaches in this study explained that there were entire lists and combinations of words that were only relevant to specific positions and players. Different positions and players might pay attention to different words based on the calls. As some words used in play calls focused on alignment, whereas others were focused on movement, players needed to know exactly which words they should attend to and then what they needed to do as a result. In addition, Coach Dean explained that different positions were trained to know which words were connected to their position. Knowing terminology was a key component of his coaching. In our interview, he explained a few basic concepts that were connected to terms that players had to understand early on:

- Personnel—the players on the field for the play
- Motion—players going in motion before the ball snaps

- Formation—how the players line up
- Play—what happens after the ball is snapped
- Trades—when a player moves from one spot to another before the ball is snapped

These basic concepts were attached to specific words that coaches would call out or signal from the sidelines. Certain words or letters were related to personnel, others were related to motion, and others described formation. Players had to know which words represented each concept and then act accordingly. As such, it was important that players on the team knew, understood, and could apply those words and signals to their role and/or position on the team. According to Coach Dean, when those offensive calls were made, every single one of the players on the field had to know what they meant and what to do, otherwise, everything would break down.

Like the other coaches in this study, Coach Todd explained that there were a number of specific terms and cues that his defensive line players needed to understand to execute plays. Get off, blitzing, changing gaps, stunts, and coverage are a few of the terms Coach Todd shared, and of course, he talked about how they used numbers to talk about coverage. Like other coaches, he shared that some words were universal, but others were specific to certain coaches and teams. Many of the words that Coach Todd shared were exclusive to the defensive line and only applied to the specific group of players he coached. In essence, football vocabulary could be broken down into different subsets of words. While there was a set that was universal and was used across the team as a whole, other pockets of words were smaller subsets that only applied to a specific set of players. This specific terminology was emphasized by Coach Leon who shared words such as gut, gap scheme, saints, squeeze, and base, but he also explained that not all players had to know all parts of a play that was called. Of course, this was different for a quarterback who had to know the entire meaning. Other players only listened out for specific words.

> Some of the stuff is just some verbiage is different depending on what position you play. So like a wide receiver could care less about Ricky and Louie. That's a pass protection. But he does care about the route. Like the wide receiver is worried about chill or quick or 1234 draw but a lineman is not worried about that. He's just worried about the pass protection. So it's a lot of stuff up there but outside of the quarterback, I don't have to know all that and we try to take some of that off of the quarterback. That's why we call Ricky or Louis, so he knows what the protection is; we take it off his plate. A wide receiver is not worried about the tags other than bunch, and nasty and close. So he's got his tags, our running backs are worried about king, queen, eye, ear, pistol, and strong. So he's not worried about every single tag up there. So our running back coach, our wide receiver coach, they're teaching their group what they need to know.

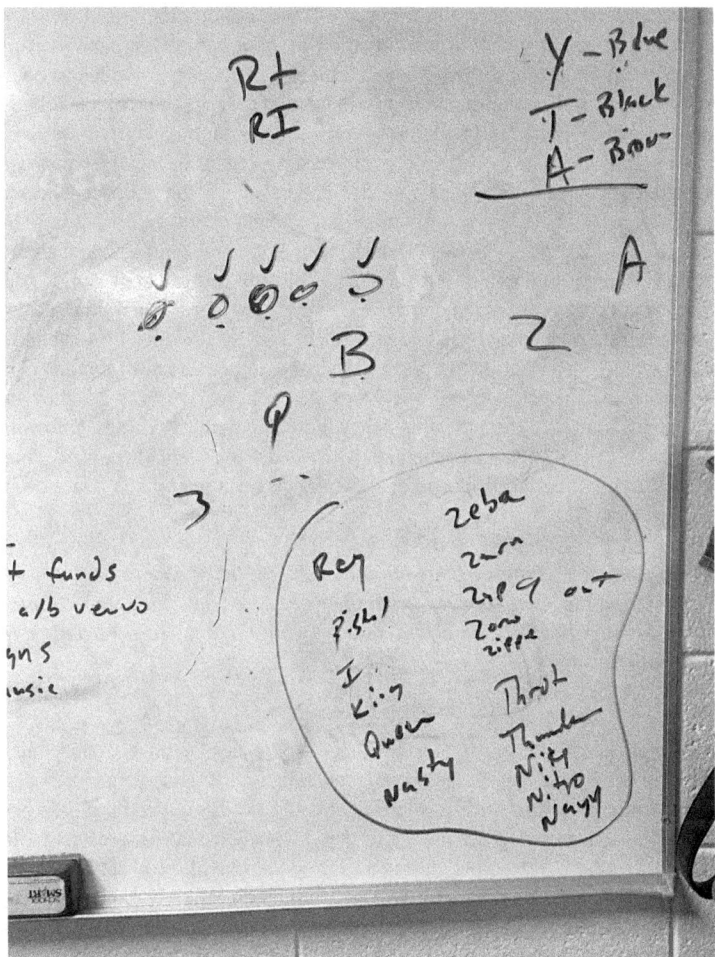

Figure 4.2 Play Diagram and Terms

Like my experiences with the other coaches, my interview with Coach Leon felt like it was part English and part foreign language. Yet the players and coaches were fluent in this language that I did not yet understand, and in many cases, had never heard before. However, they knew which words were meant for certain players and the purpose and action associated with each (See Figure 4.2).

This specific attention to certain words based on purpose and the role of the player is closely connected to what is present in the academic classroom. Think about constructed response prompts in multiple disciplines. For students to successfully complete a constructed response prompt, they need to know what key words they should pay attention to along with what each word is asking them to do. For example, when a prompt includes words such as compare, explain, and prove, students must know that they will be looking at more than one item (compare), they must give an explanation (explain) of the comparisons, and they cite evidence (prove) that supports the answer. Not knowing what one of those words means, or not understanding the action connected to it, can cause a student to provide an incomplete or incorrect answer. The same result might happen when a player does not know what a specific word requires him/her to do on the field, which can result in a failed execution of a play. What coaches are doing on the field as it relates to vocabulary instruction is closely related to what might be implemented in an academic classroom. In fact, I would argue that the purpose is the same: to get students to understand the action or concept assigned to a word. As such, teachers and coaches are reinforcing similar skills and competency in their individual settings. Knowing how complex the language of their sports is, Coach Wes remarked, "I feel like if you can get this (the language of football), you can get what's going on in the classroom."

> *Words matter. But on Friday night they might not be able to hear us yelling. So at the same time we teach the words, we teach the signals. Come Friday nights, that's what they see. We want them to learn verbally and visually.*
> —*Coach Dean*

Words were not the only type of language used in these settings. Coaches also relied on symbols, gestures, and sounds for communication. In some instances, athletes might be in a setting where they could not hear specific words, so, instead, coaches used other means of communication that were effective in those instances. For example, during a swim meet, one of the coaches utilized a series of specific whistles and whoops to communicate directions to swimmers who were racing in the pool and could not see their coaches. These sounds were a form of language utilized in the race setting where words and gestures would not have been effective. Athletes needed to have a solid understanding of this "language" as well to know how they should respond. Because of the instruction that occurred previously in their practice setting, swimmers knew which whistles and which whoops meant different actions. To the observer in the stands, these noises simply sounded like a cheering coach, but for the swimmer in the water, it was a specific direction communicated through another type of auditory language.

Other forms of signs were utilized in swimming on a regular basis. During long-distance swimming, lap counters are utilized so that swimmers do not swim too much or not enough, which is especially important in races such as the 1,000-meter or 1,650-meter freestyle. In distance swimming, swimmers even know what they should do based on how the counter is agitated in the water. If a coach wants a swimmer to pick up the pace, the person holding the counter shakes it rapidly under the water, whereas, if the swimmer needs to keep up their current pace, the counter is simply held steady in the water (See Figure 4.3).

Similarly, signals instead of words are used on game nights, so the football players have to know not only the word but also the sign for each. Coaches explained that, while there were specific words that were used in practice, they did not just rely on words to convey information. In fact, many utilized signals and hand gestures to convey a directive. This was especially beneficial during game time or race time when athletes might be limited by what they could hear on the field or court. In fact, Coach Wayne explained that, on game nights, they relied almost exclusively on signals and signs to communicate their instruction. The quarterback's responsibility was to make certain he saw the sign from the sideline and then communicate it to the lineman.

On game nights, there were three football coaches all throwing up signs from the sideline, but only one of them was "hot" meaning only one was giving the true directions. The other two coaches are used as distractors for the opposing team; however, prior to game night, the players all know which coach is really giving the instruction. Starting on Monday, they practice this component as well so that the players know where they should train their eyes on Friday night. Like other teams, Coach Todd's team utilizes decoys who are throwing up irrelevant signs which helps to confuse the other team. This is typically done

Figure 4.3 Lap Counters in Swim Race

by having three coaches on the sidelines giving signals, but only one of them is really calling the plays. Players have to know which coach is "hot" meaning that they are the one who is giving out the true signs.

These signs have solid connections to semiotics and reading, as semiotics is essentially the study and examination of signs and signifiers (Peirce & Buchler, 2011). These signs and signifiers are prevalent in multiple settings and are often used when verbal communication might not be possible. In fact, several years ago when visiting a café in New Orleans, I watched a worker place utensils in specific positions on customers' trays based on what they ordered. As the tray traveled down the line, another worker was able to look at how the silverware was positioned and would place a specific food item on the tray. For example, a spoon lying face up at the top of the tray might mean the customer ordered a coffee, whereas a fork flipped upside down on the right-hand side of the tray might indicate they placed an order for beignets. Without speaking to each other, the workers were able to communicate with each other. In this example, individuals who are part of a specific context have developed another communication system in addition to oral language. This form of communication has a specific function, and its own set of rules (a spoon here means this) to convey meaning (Harper, 2014). However, beyond that, it is specifically ground in the context in which the language and symbols are used. Much like what the coaches described in their explanations of their words, sounds, and gestures that are connected to their specific sports, these non-athletic real-world examples are no different.

Written words only have any relevance or connections when they are associated with a concept or idea. In essence, written words on paper mean nothing until there is meaning associated with them. Thus, Coach Wayne's "Bama," Coach Gary's "T drill," and Coach Dean's "Racket, Base" are lost if the athlete does not understand what is meant by the word or gesture. Closely connected to comprehension, students who can word call but do not know what words mean, struggle with comprehension. Word calling is essentially when an individual can pronounce or say a word, but they do not know what the word means. Without understanding the meaning behind the word, comprehension suffers.

Coach Wayne explained that he often observed players who transferred from other teams demonstrate a lack of understanding of some of the words or terms his coaches might use. However, when they saw the action that was associated with the word, the players immediately caught on and were able to connect the action to a new word or phrase. In numerous instances, coaches were observed modeling the action and then connecting a specific word or phrase to that action.

Much like the other sports addressed in this manuscript, basketball included its own vocabulary, terminology, and expressions. Coach Aaron explained there were many basketball words and terms that his players had to know to be successful. Words such as press, box out, and rebound were frequently used, and players had to know what these meant to execute a specific play or drill. Similarly, baseline, in the paint, and box out were often used by Coach Cathy in interviews as she explained how in some drills athletes did not need to "dribble in the middle of the paint," "make them go baseline," or "box out," which I often had to ask her to explain. Many of her explanations involved her showing me what that word meant by demonstrating the action. In fact, many times without my asking, she automatically began demonstrating while she used words to explain. Many of these words were brand new to me, however, in observations of practice, these words were frequently used, and all players knew exactly what was meant when these expressions or words were used. While some may have started the year not knowing what they meant, practice, modeling, and explanations of the actions that accompanied the words helped cement understanding for players and made it easier for them to not only comprehend what was being asked but also help them as they utilized them in their own communications with players.

Coach Hugh explained how important communication and language were for their team's success. He went on to share that, in some instances, they could give players a word or phrase that would dictate multiple actions needed from the player. "Football is all about language. I use the term 'Come to power,' and that phrase dictates about five things they're supposed to do. So it's its own language." During this explanation, Coach Hugh brought in a player to demonstrate exactly what that term meant. As the coach said that command, the player immediately performed the action. Coach Hugh explained,

> So his feet went from long to a narrow stance. He went from taking long strides to short strides. He went from a vertical where his shoulders are over his hips, so now his shoulders are over his knees. He went from being upright to bending at three locations: ankle, knees, and hip.

That in itself was fascinating-that one phrase, "Come to power," would result in multiple actions. However, perhaps even more fascinating was how quickly it occurred. In a second or fraction thereof, the player completed those actions quickly, effectively, and instinctively. This player's response was natural and immediate; there was not any confusion in the directions or in the task.

These observations reminded me of my own children's experience in primary classrooms as they learned to read. In my daughter Amelia's kindergarten class, her teacher utilized symbols (letters), sounds, and gestures to remind students about specific letter sounds. For example, when students practiced the letter B, they would stand up, say, "B" and then make the B sound while pretending to swing a bat. Her teacher explained to me that using the gestures offered her an additional opportunity for instruction. If a student was struggling with how to spell a word and the teacher was observing from across the room, she could signal the student with the gesture which could trigger a reminder for the individual student. When conducting this research, I thought back to that academic example which in essence is exactly what they coaches are implementing in their sports setting.

Aside from the sports-specific vocabulary, there were also multiple instances where coaches were utilizing other academic terminology that is often present in the classroom. For example, Coach Cathy often told her players to turn 90 degrees or make a 180-degree turn on the court. She referenced a right triangle and explained player placement in terms of angles. When giving these directives, no players stopped and asked for an explanation; instead, they knew exactly where to go and what angle they should utilize to make certain they made the basket.

While most of the players knew a lot of the basketball terminology ahead of time, Coach Cathy explained that she would often check for understanding. "I will actually say and go to them and say, 'Do you understand what this it?'" When players could not articulate the answer or give the appropriate explanation, Coach Cathy utilized different techniques to address this. In some cases, she would work individually with players, whereas, at other times, she would pull the whole team off to the side and give a new demonstration. Acronyms were also used when communicating to players which served as another form of language and vocabulary.

Knowing what the words meant was only part of it. Several of the coaches emphasized the importance of players communicating using the language of the sport. When discussing the terminology used, Coach Todd explained that they want their players to give specifics about where they need to go or what direction the need to block or pass. Knowing exactly what area they were supposed to cover helped players perform on Friday and those specific details (cover the A gap) helped players know the specifics of their actions and instructions. Instead of saying, "I need to cover that gap over there," players were encouraged and sometimes required to specifically describe where they needed to go or what they needed to do by using the appropriate language. Thus, if a player was supposed to cover a certain gap, they had to refer to the gap with its correct name (A, B, C, etc.). This specificity of language, instructions, and explanations helped coaches to continue to reinforce the language of the sport on a regular basis. Instead of asking a player to give them a definition of an A gap, coaches expected players to be able to define that A gap by explaining where it was, who would cover it, and why that was the expectation.

While words are often used to represent actions and concepts, numbers are also employed and used to explain field position and lineup.

> When they communicate about the lineup, we teach them numbers. It is just a common language for us to speak. Like if a player says, "Well, Coach, he's

(opposing player) in front of me." What's that mean? Like where is he? So we teach them lined up in the front they are a one, handle is a two, outside shoulder is a three, inside shoulder is a four, head up is a five, outside shoulder is a six, head up field is a zero.

Coach Wayne explained that this was very valuable information to a coach because they could not see everything from the sideline. When players could tell the coaches that an opposing player was lined up at a two or four, that gave the coaches valuable information that they could use to make game decisions. Coach Cedric shared that his players often used numbers when communicating on the court because the numbers represented their alignment on the court. During practice, they would run specific drills and then discuss them using pertinent terminology and numbers. Coach Wes echoed this sentiment as he believed that language is learned through repetition.

We force them out here to talk to us in our language. You don't get away with just pointing; tell me where you are going. So if I am responsible for the A gap, don't just tell me 'I got this gap.' You tell me I got A gap. We don't let them off the hook.

He explained that, even if the player was initially wrong, talking through the event using the terminology allowed coaches to continue their instruction and correct any misconceptions.

It's all done through repetition. To get these kids to understand this terminology it's a bunch of repetition. So they understand when we speak our language. When you talk to us, talk to us using our language.
—*Coach Wes*

Learning the words associated with each sport was not something that occurred overnight and instead involved prolonged instruction that evolved throughout the course of a season. Both Coach Neal and Hugh believed that some players came to them with a foundation in the vocabulary used, but it was not a significant number. Most of the learning of these discipline-specific words came from the instruction the coaches provided. For example, the vast amount of football vocabulary that was present in Coach Dean's practice required explicit teaching as many of the terms were team-specific. He explained that they started out with a few terms and then gradually added more once the players were proficient in the initial ones. By the time the football season rolled around in August, the players had a large repertoire in their lexicon. "Words matter," but when it comes to Friday night, players had to know signals too. If a play is called with three words, now players must also know the three signals for those words. Players need to know what each word means, but, perhaps more importantly, they must know what each word dictates that they do. Football coaches worked to use consistent clues in their words which in some cases meant that the words that addressed field position or direction corresponded to that direction. For example, words that all meant left started with L, whereas those that focused on the right side of the field started with the letter R.

Coach Cedric explained that, early in the season, he began by identifying the basics of basketball vocabulary including the names for the different parts of the basketball court including the free throw line, wings, block, and three-point line. Like the other coaches, he explained that there were some terms that were labeled differently by other teams or coaches, but the basics he started with were fairly universal.

Coach Dan explained that instruction at the beginning of the season often included the use of videos to help demonstrate proper technique but also aided in the introduction of the language of swimming. Keywords were often used when providing feedback to swimmers as well. Words and phrases such as threshold, catch up, taper, high elbows, streamline, and glide were frequently used, and Coach Dan explained that, when teaching these new words initially, he often used whiteboards, videos, and handouts so that swimmers could have multiple examples of the term and concept. Incorporating these terms during feedback sessions required the swimmers to self-assess and have a keen sense of awareness regarding their performance. For example, when Coach Dan used terms such as threshold plus or threshold minus, those words gave the athletes the cue for how fast they should swim their sets. This was similar to what Coach Nate described when he gave swimmers instructions on their practice pace. He often used words along with percentages.

> You know, and I think that really comes down to the coaches being ok, hey, when we talk about smooth, think about, I like to use percentages. You know, I say, hey, when you think smooth think 80% effort or if they're still not getting it, it's ok. Smooth is, is just faster than warm up, it's relaxed, it's clean, ok? Strong is you're moving just fast enough that the coaches aren't going to be upset at you, but you're still going to make your interval, right?

Coach Dan also explained that, on the team website, they kept a glossary or handbook of the terms they used in swimming. This was often a helpful aid for parents who might not know what each of the terms meant or who may have children who were new to swimming. While there were certain words that were foundational in each sport, Coach Elliott shared that they also worked on teaching the athletes the different variations that might be connected to each word. In addition, like Coach Alex, Coach Elliott believed that explaining the why behind the word and action was important as well. As the season progressed, Coach Elliott and his colleagues might add additional terms and phrases, but only after the foundation was built.

This progression was explained by Coach Gary, who asserted that, by September or October, all he had to do was cue the swimmers and give them a quick word or phrase and they knew what they needed to do. Sometimes, he might even show them a gesture, "When they are swimming, I can show them an elbow bent and they can make that change on the fly."

Many of the coaches shared that efficiency in their instruction was one of the most important aspects of their vocabulary integration and teaching. Because they needed to provide as much information as possible in a short window of time, Coach Gary and his staff utilized a number of codes and shorthand so they could deliver the material as quickly and efficiently as possible.

> I'll spend some time when things get rough, going over a deep explanation of it. But hopefully, the time we spend on the deep stuff pays off because going forward all I'm going to do is the shortcut and give them tips. Just saying a key word that reminds them of that thing.

In practice, many of these commands or instructions were given during practice sets, most often when the swimmers were coming into the wall and resting on their intervals. During the time on the wall, Coach Gary explained that, due to the short duration of time at rest, he might only say a short word or phrase and the swimmers knew what they needed to do next. "I can just say the word, 'skills' and they know that means. For example, when I say, 'Discipline skills,' they know they need to stop breathing." These skills referred to a number of swimming concepts and techniques, including starts, turns, underwaters, and other little details that could improve swimming performance.

Much like other sports, swimming has its own glossary of terms that were used frequently in practice. Because many of these words are not ones that the athletes were using in their regular worlds, introducing the terminology early was key. Coach Gary also emphasized how important it was for parents to understand that acquiring these new skills was not going to happen overnight because, essentially, they were having to learn a new language.

> Even if they are coming from another established team, we are going to switch it up. Like we are going to call the exact same drill that you did over there something different. Like last night I was talking to Coach Shannon and we were talking about human free drills and she calls it "Big Dog." So it is all the same: mimic doggy paddles, but she calls it Big Dog and I called it human. So our coaches are going to try to make sure that we are using the same syntax.

Time with the swimmers helped them build and learn the vocabulary and repetition was key for comprehension. It was not unusual to hear Coach Gary barking out drills such as 50T, 25S, and 75F, which he later explained to me meant:

> Each stroke has a specific drill for each of the letters T, S, and F. 50 T stands for a technical drill, 25 S is a speed drill, and 75 F is a focus drill. In each of these drills, they focus on specific items. For example, technical drills highlight technique in a stroke and usually break down the stroke into parts. For a speed drill, these are short bursts of speed-focused drills that focus on speed of the arms and getting the swimmer's heart rate up. Focus drill is one that focuses on rhythm. They can usually do it for long distances and it usually feels like the full stroke with a slight twist to make it a drill. It is a more cohesive drill and is a kind of a combination of the T drill and the actually regular swimming of the stroke.

While Coach Gary used a whiteboard to help teach the terms and the substitutions, he explained that, for each skill level, he had a cut-off where he wanted the swimmers to have the terms and substitutions memorized in their heads (See Figure 4.4).

So much of what each coach explained made my head swim. It was a vocabulary and concept overload for someone who had limited experiences in these settings. Throughout this research study, I reflected on how many students

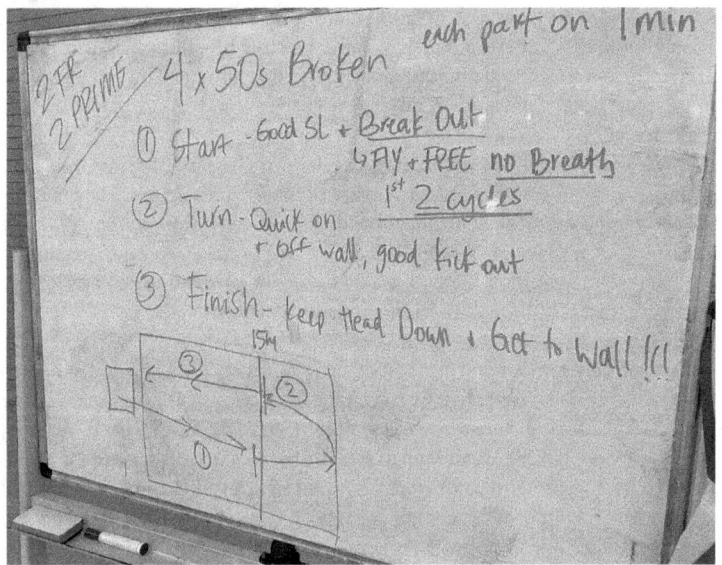

Figure 4.4 Swim Practice Plan

might feel when they are met with a new concept and a difficult task. In some cases, it would be easier to simply throw your hands up and quit, especially when overwhelmed, which is how I felt multiple times as I combed through the terminology, diagrams, and interviews. In my interview with Coach Max, he threw out so many vocabulary terms that I could not even begin to think of what question I might start with. However, what I noticed again was that each coach in their explanations used words, gestures, and written diagrams as a means of instruction. Thus, when Coach Max rattled off words such as lion, zipper, zulu, pistol, eye, king, and queen, for example, he explained them through physical demonstration and diagrams on the white board. In many instances, he was on his feet mimicking the motion or stance that he might assume on the football field. Thus, it was not just an oral or written definition of a word; it was a multifaceted definition that helped cement understanding.

At one point during an interview with a football coach, I stood in front of a whiteboard with dozens of words and phrase combinations that essentially represented multiple directions and concepts. My first feeling was one of inadequacy; I could read every one of the words, but I did not know what any of them meant. I wondered if this is how many of our students feel in the academic classroom. From an intellectual standpoint, my inability to decipher what was posted on the board was not a reflection of my intelligence, but rather one on my inexperience and lack of exposure. However, I am an adult with a lifetime of experience in education and a Ph.D. in Language and Literacy, thus I recognized early that my inability to comprehend what was written on the white board was not indicative of my intelligence. Yet I imagine that some young adolescents may not recognize that their lack of comprehension for a subject or concept is directly linked to their background knowledge and experience and not necessarily their intelligence level. Thus, some students may elect to shut down due to their frustration. How might we get students to understand this and recognize that they do not necessarily lack the ability, but rather the experience and exposure? (See Figure 4.5).

Throughout my coding and writing, I found myself sending texts to the coaches in this study, with Coach Elliott taking the brunt of my questions when I was confused by the words in my transcripts. On a regular basis, I would send clarifying questions, and in some cases, I had more questions than answers. I felt like I was asking the same questions over and over, "Remind me how the defensive players line up, Coach Elliott. What is a stunt?" And then I thought about how our students must feel in academic classrooms sometimes. "What does she mean by counterclaim? How am I supposed to cite evidence?"

In thinking on this, I realized that, through my own experience in this research study, I was slowly becoming more proficient in sports vocabulary. How? Through exposure, repetition, and application. The more I heard a word used in context along with demonstrations and explanations, I began to understand it on a deeper level. Diagrams and sketches that coaches utilized in their explanations were key in my own understanding as this gave me another layer

68   Third Quarter

Figure 4.5 Football Plays

of understanding: a word, an oral explanation, and a visual accompaniment. When explaining terminology to me, Coach Elliott, like most of the others in this study often pulled out paper and pencil to show diagrams or draw what he was explaining. Vocabulary lessons often were accompanied by drawing pictures and candid explanations with possible scenarios and other extensions to fully explain a concept (See Figure 4.6).

However, here is what else happened. While writing, I found that my understanding was at its peak when I did the following:

- Held multiple interviews the same week.
- Watched practice immediately before or after an interview.
- Read my interview transcript soon after the actual interview.
- Began writing soon after the interview.

On the occasions when I had spaces of time between my visits to the field and my actual writing, I noticed that I had more questions about what I read in my transcripts and included in my notes. Why? Think about experience and exposure. On those weeks where I was in multiple research settings, I was able to see and experience these concepts on a repeated basis, and in multiple settings. If I interviewed Coach Elliott, Coach Wayne, and Coach Todd all in one week, I had repeated exposure to a similar set of concepts and words because they all

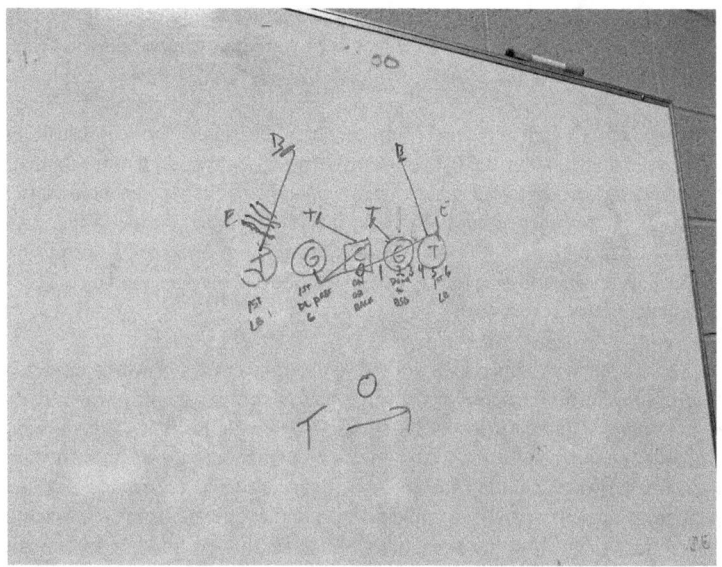

Figure 4.6 Football Play

coach football. Thus, by my third interview that week, when one of them used the term "gap," I knew what that was because of my previous repeated experience. However, outside of my data collection, I was not hearing or using these words on a regular basis, so when I was not actively collecting data or writing about it, I was not using those words.

Now let us think about our students in the classroom. How often are there specific words that might be used in the fifth period, but only fifth period? What about words that only are used in the fifth period at a certain time of the semester? Do you see how it might be more difficult to retain that material than if a student used a specific set of words in multiple classes on a daily basis? For words and their meanings to stick, they must be part of the individual's world. Otherwise, in many instances, there is limited knowledge retention.

Despite their unique attributes and sport-specific characteristics, each one had an extended list of words and phrases employed. Coach Elliott talked about how complex the terminology and components of football are and he showed me playbooks that were hundreds of pages long. He recounted players who might read on a fourth-grade reading level, but who could memorize entire playbooks and hundreds of words related to the game. Why could they do this on the field but not so much in the classroom? Coach Elliott chalks it up to motivation and interest. This was related to Coach Dean's discussion about how in some ways, the motivation to play the game spurred students to perform better in the classroom even if they did not want to. While they might not be motivated to learn the academic content, they were motivated to play in Friday night's game.

> There's more light at the end of the tunnel in their eyes. Football is learning Romeo and Juliet or the Pythagorean Theorem. I got to do that for football. I have to keep my grades up. Coach wants me to lift weights hard and he wants me to practice hard after I do that. He's gonna put me in the game on Friday night. I might score a touchdown, and everybody can put me on Facebook. And you know, I'm just talking about teenage boys. That's human nature.

These noticings helped as I worked to determine ways in which academic teachers might utilize some of the same tactics coaches employ when teaching vocabulary in their respective settings. Along with this, how can educators make the connections so that the athletes recognize that the same skills they utilize in the practice setting are employed in the academic classroom? Taking a page from a coach's playbook could have a number of benefits in the academic classroom. Aside from the vocabulary strategies implemented in the athletic setting, the instructional methods for building foundational skills were significant and their continued focus on these basics long after mastery had apparent benefits. Transferring some of these tactics into the academic classroom could provide more opportunities for prolonged learning and skill-building in numerous content areas outside of athletics.

5 Fourth Quarter
No Fumbles on Feedback

You don't ever want to stop trying to make them better players. You always gotta keep trying to get them to be better.
—Coach Wayne

It is well known in instructional settings that feedback is important for growth and improvement (Hattie & Timperley, 2007; Hattie & Ziere, 2019; Sadler, 2010). While the inclusion of feedback is important for classroom instruction, progress, and improvement, the frequency and manner in which it is delivered are equally important. Data collected in this study indicated that the feedback cycle in coaching had some significant differences from that of feedback in the classroom. My time in educational settings for over 20 years yielded some observations regarding feedback that were significantly different from the methods coaches employed with their feedback. In typical classroom instruction, aside from informal feedback that might be given to a student through questioning, reinforcement, or monitoring, most formal feedback comes with a significant delay, which is often observable in formal assessments and testing. Consider how students are traditionally assessed. In many instances, they are given a test or other assessment that is often graded and returned at a later date, thus delaying the feedback on student performance. When it comes to standardized tests, this delay in returned feedback is even more pronounced, as many Advanced Placement tests, state assessments, and other high-stakes assessments are often not returned until the next quarter or school year. By the time students receive their feedback, many may have forgotten what was addressed in the assessment. In addition, in most instances, the feedback provided does not always include a plan of action for exactly *what* to do with the feedback received. Goals may or may not be a part of the assessment process, and in some instances, students might not have input in the articulation of goals. In fact, in most classrooms, teachers rely on curriculum standards and pacing guides to develop and plan their instruction, assessment, and teaching goals.

Unlike these classroom observations, data from the participants in this study indicate that coaching feedback was most often:

- Individualized
- Immediate
- Utilized multiple modalities
- Was ongoing and progressive
- Was tethered to athlete performance

Regardless of the sport, these characteristics were common in all settings. While the setting might vary, whether it was on the field, court, or pool, athletes were the recipients of consistent and individualized feedback regardless of skill level, performance, or training cycle. In addition, their feedback often took on multiple forms and was presented through a variety of modalities. These features assisted coaches in executing a feedback protocol and cycle that was most effective in their respective settings.

> *I mean it's constant. The feedback comes as they are going down the field sometimes. It's constant feedback.*
> —***Coach Elliott***

When it comes to feedback in the coaching setting, in most instances, feedback was almost immediate whether it was during practice or a game. During football games, as soon as the players came off the field, they met with their coaches to receive information and commentary on their performance. Coach Wes explained that, on Friday nights, televisions and tents were set up so players could immediately see video evidence of what was occurring on the field.

> We go back and check for understanding during the game. Like, "Alright, this is what we got. Everybody sees what happened? You see why we wanted to do this? Alright this is what they are trying to do to us. You see why we cannot do that?" So they get a chance to see what we practiced during the week. They get a chance to correct themselves during the course of a game.

Coach Wes explained that this feature was important for game nights since players were not only able to receive oral feedback from their coaches right after a play, but they could also see a visual example or text. Like Coach Wes, Coach Todd shared that feedback in many instances was almost instantaneous which allowed players and coaches to immediately correct mistakes. Because of the software and filming capacity that was available, Coach Todd and his players could see the plays from the current game while on the sideline. Each coaching staff member had an iPad which they used to show players video footage on demand. Like Coach Wes shared, coaches and players had a television located in a covered tent area and could pull up plays or a series of plays which allowed them to give almost immediate feedback to their players. While Coach Todd shared that giving this type of feedback on the fly did not allow him to correct it as thoroughly as when he was able to view film in a more controlled setting, it did give him and the players the opportunities to immediately correct small mistakes during the game so that they might have a better outcome. This technology allowed them to correct multiple components live and during the game. Thus, the delay for feedback was limited.

In addition, because game night tended to be fast-paced, having multiple modalities for delivering feedback was helpful simply due to the nature of the game. During game time, especially in team sports like basketball, feedback was happening almost like rapid fire, in quick bursts of information due to the rapid intensity of the game. While in the game, it might be a little more difficult to stop everything and provide extensive feedback, Coach Ty said coaches would often yell out from the sidelines feedback to individual players. This feedback might be as simple as positive reinforcement or it might be more direct and specific, but providing feedback to players was something that was done on a consistent and regular basis.

Similarly, Coach Dean explained that his feedback on Friday nights sometimes varied based on the situation.

> If we see it and we have a chance to talk to the guy, we do. Sometimes we see it and we go from offense to defense and the guy is playing both ways and he goes from offense and he stays on the field and we don't have a chance to talk to him. When he comes to the sideline, we'll tell him. The other part is we may not see it till after the game on Sunday when we look at the film.

For those opportunities where a coach could correct something during game night, Coach Dean explained they made every effort to do so. However, when teams have a limited roster and their players play multiple positions, sometimes there may be a delay in this communication. Regardless, by Monday, the players had received some form of feedback from their coaches on their game or race performance. Like other football coaches in this study, Coach Hugh and Neal shared that much of the feedback that players received on Friday nights was instant and also included video evidence and examples as they had access to film on the sidelines which allowed them to make corrections in real time and adjust on the spot.

For Coach Alan's swimmers, feedback was immediate, but immediate was relative and depended on the setting. For example, during a swim meet "immediate" meant as soon as the swimmer came up to the coach after a race or a warm-down. However, during practice, "immediate" might be at the end of a set.

> Sometimes when I see a swimmer who needs to be corrected on a stroke, I will watch that stroke and maybe not interrupt the set because it's a heart

rate set. Stopping them would basically ruin the set for them. But if it's something that is drastic and just completely needs to be addressed, it will be immediate.

For Coach Alan, determining the most appropriate time to offer feedback was especially important because of several factors. In some cases, waiting till the end of the set or practice was best, whereas at other times, he needed to stop the swimmer and offer corrective feedback right away. Similarly, sometimes, Coach Wayne wanted feedback during practice to come later. This often occurred when they were playing their best on best during practice because he simply wanted them to play fast. In this case, feedback came the next day when the players watched the plays on film and then discussed their observations. While the feedback was not exactly immediate, the delay was minimal, and because Coach Wayne accompanied his commentary with video evidence as a reference text, the visual footage helped activate the players' prior knowledge and served as a reminder of the prior days' events.

Coach Dan attempted to talk with swimmers and provide feedback in between sets or during downtime so that they could see what components they were doing well, and which ones needed improvement. He emphasized that using keywords was especially important because those were the words that the swimmers were most accustomed to based on the instruction they had received throughout the season. In addition, as Coach Gary explained in an interview, he needed to provide feedback in the most efficient manner possible. Time spent training was precious and so coaches often looked to provide commentary and suggestions in the most efficient ways possible.

Coaches in this study shared that, while feedback was a core component of their practice, knowing when to provide this commentary was an important consideration for an effective exchange. In many instances, coaches had to determine whether or not the setting allowed for feedback delivery, whereas, in other instances, recognizing the needs of the athletes helped coaches determine when this conversation was appropriate. In doing so, coaches continued to individualize and tailor their instruction and feedback for each player. In addition, because many coaches relied on a variety of supplemental texts (videos, recordings, and diagrams), athletes were able to comprehend and process the feedback in a comprehensive manner.

> *It's videos, verbal, paper, and we show them visually. They get auditory and then they get it visually again by putting it on paper and showing it to them.*
>
> —**Coach Wes**

Not only were coaches cognizant of when feedback should be provided, but they also focused on how they might deliver constructive criticism or praise. Because much of the feedback that coaches provided addressed areas for improvement or refinement, it was important that coaches deliver messages in the most effective manner possible. While athletic skills were demonstrated physically and also called out verbally, Coach Dean emphasized the importance of being specific on what players needed to do when providing instruction. Giving the athletes specific directives, but also being cognizant of the type of delivery needed for different player personalities was important. According to Coach Dean, sometimes this direction varied based on the player and the coach. In some instances, coaches came down hard on players, whereas, in other instances, they utilized more positive feedback components. Knowing which players would respond to hard criticism versus one who might shut down helped coaches determine how and when to deliver feedback. Coach Max explained that this also involved a balance between a lot of criticism along with a strategy for improvement coupled with the best way to present the information to the athlete. In addition, Coach Wes shared that feedback was provided visually, verbally, with videos, on paper, and with demonstrations. And Coach Leon would provide feedback by physically modeling what was expected.

> We go out there and show them. You know, we'll line up and say, "Hey, this is where you're at. So how do we line up. Alright, now we're running this route. I need you to get here. Alright, quarterback, you're looking at this defender-here's your one read, here's your two read." We do a lot of that. And then obviously the majority of what we do it rep, rep, rep, rep, which is practice, practice, practice.

Other coaches explained that feedback sometimes looked different based on the player and the individual needs of the athletes, and it sometimes was dependent on the progression of the season. For example, Coach Cathy recalled an example in practice where one of her players was not performing:

> Yesterday we were in practice and I have two particular (players) who don't box out well and so they are down there they are boxing out so it's going fine so then the two people switched so it got harder for one of them and she just shut down. I mean it was like, "Wow. What! Now you got competition, and you don't want to compete so you are going to let her have the ball." I mean when I say she would just stop and not even put forth that effort and my thought process is that's how you are in the classroom, ya' know, because of the correlation, if it gets hard, she shuts down, but if it's easy, I can do it. So I talked to her after practice and I told her you can't shut down like you got to keep going. Life is going to be hard. You're going to learn a lot of life lessons in basketball that you can relate to when you leave here.

Speaking with that athlete one-on-one after practice helped Coach Cathy connect with her player and determine how to provide her with the type of feedback that can help that player improve her performance. That same player, Coach Cathy went on to explain, had a difficult time after receiving that constructive criticism from her the day before and did not initially know how to interact with her after the previous day's practice. She explained:

> So now today she needed some help with a study guide, so she sent one of the other players in here to ask me for help and I said, "Nope; it doesn't work like that. She has to come in here and ask for help." She (the player) peeped around the door and I was like, "I slept well last night. I didn't think about what happened in practice yesterday. When I came home I was able to separate the two and I need you to do the same thing. You come in here and I will give you some help." But this attitude of you're not doing what you are supposed to do and you get mad, but I'm not bringing it to the next day-that's not how I operate. Every day is different, and we got to move forward.

Different players required different types of feedback and Coach Cathy explained that she could not use the same tactics with every player. For example, she explained how some players she can come down on harder than others because other players simply would shut down. One of her most dedicated players was one she could get on to, and that player, no matter what, would do whatever she asked her to do.

> She's the first one at practice, always has the basketball, and is going to do everything I ask. Ya know, I can get on her and she is like, "Okay, whatever," but she is always trying to do what I need her to do.

The feedback that Coach Cathy provided her players, regardless of the delivery, was meant to help them improve their performance.

Coach Aaron explained that some players responded better to positive feedback, while others needed more constructive criticism and firm feedback. In some instances, the feedback he provided was related to their academic endeavors. While Coach Aaron acknowledged that some of his players struggled academically, he explained that he tried to help motivate his players by reminding them about their eligibility and what that meant for them individually and for the entire team.

> I tell them if you get to a point where you are not able to play, you are not hurting me—you are hurting the team. I want you to play and we need you, but if you are not going to take care of the classroom, you cannot be on the court.

Post-game discussion with Coach Aaron often included a lot of self-reflection, with players explaining and critiquing their performance and giving suggestions for improvement and adjustment. This self-reflection often aided Coach Aaron in helping players formulate goals and make plans for the season. In addition, it allowed the players to provide feedback and commentary on their own performance on a regular and routine basis.

Like other coaches in the study, feedback differed based on the athlete as Coach Todd explained that some players needed more positive reinforcement, whereas others needed to be broken down to build them up. When breaking down film with players, Coach Todd explained that there was a mixture of positive reinforcement along with criticism of what needed to be addressed going forward. This form of feedback helped players by acknowledging their strengths but also gave them items that needed individual attention since they were given feedback that helped them adjust and improve their practice.

Similarly, Coach Wayne described coaching in this way:

> I am trying to take a player from where he sees himself to where he could be. I wanna see that through. Having fun. I wanna see that though showing each other respect. I wanna see that through encouragement. The more we can encourage and show respect and have fun, the better they are gonna be.

For Coach Wayne, coaching and providing feedback to players were not all about breaking a player down, but rather helping him or her see their full potential and then find the means to be successful.

By providing feedback along the way, many coaches believed that this helped their athletes improve their self-confidence and become more confident in asking questions.

In swimming, instruction and feedback were ongoing as Coach Gary explained that coaches were trying to give swimmers as much information as possible in a short amount of time. This meant that even when swimmers were at the wall waiting on an interval or taking a short break between a set, coaches were providing feedback or direction on what they should focus on in the next set.

Similarly, in football, when watching film, there are times during the week when Coach Wayne compares it with a quiz and sight recognition. He explained that they may watch film of an opponent and then ask the players, "'What do we do when they are in this formation? What do I expect?' Now they have to communicate with us what we expect." He went on to elaborate that as the players get more comfortable and as the week goes on, more players are willing to share and give their assessments. By the time they conduct the walkthrough on Thursday, several players are giving input compared with early on in the week where they might only have a couple of volunteers. Much of this progress is related to the feedback that coaches provide throughout the week during practice which helped their players analyze film and develop questions based on their observations.

Coach Neal explained that when they gave feedback to players they asked for specifics and made certain to utilize specific and specialized directions so that players knew exactly what they should do for improvement. As explained earlier, using a common language was also important when delivering feedback as coaches needed to make certain that players were being provided consistent and uniform directives that were clear. Through the use of specific and direct feedback, players were able to identify the areas for improvement or the areas of success in their performance, all of which were scaffolded by their coaches' instructional practices. As Coach Wayne explained, modeling and feedback throughout the week aided his athletes in the articulation of questions and observational practices.

Aside from using common language and phrases for feedback, many coaches also recorded practice in addition to games and meets. Coach Hugh explained how important this was for players as filming practice and providing instant feedback improved the performance of his players. Coach Wayne indicated that, by recording practice, when his players came to school the next day and were in football class, he could show the footage from the prior day's practice or even view it at the beginning of the next practice. In this way, viewing the film became the activator for the class or practice and was used as the text from which players would be questioned. In addition, this helped his athletes who were visual learners and served as a reminder of the prior day's activities. In addition, this was helpful for his athletes who might not be on the starting lineup but might be second- or third-string players. Listening to the feedback provided to the players who were actively part of the play helped even those who were sideline observers.

Sideline cameras were not the only method used for video recording practice. Coach Wayne explained that, on some days, they flew drones over practice so that they could examine the footage from an aerial view. This helped players see more of the big picture when it came to formations and plays. Sometimes, when using the drone, Coach Wayne would ask the drone operator to focus on specific items which helped coaches and players refine specific components of their performance. In many instances, players were asked for suggestions regarding what areas or perspectives should be filmed based on their practice feedback. If players were having an issue covering a specific gap, or running a specific route, using the drone to film these items allowed the team to have a specific text dedicated to this focus area. In doing so, Coach Wayne was establishing a purpose for filming, much like readers do when they establish a purpose for reading different text types. This purposeful filming allowed Coach Wayne to target specific areas for improvement or highlight certain skills or plays that athletes were effectively performing. Because their coaching team filmed practice, players were able to view their performance on the practice field and on a more frequent basis. While the ultimate assessment was on Friday, opportunities for feedback and revision along the way were integral for performance.

> The test is always on Friday. But we show them practice film from Monday and Tuesday and the mistakes they were making on Monday when we watched that film on Wednesday they're not making that mistake no more. There's a sense of gratification.

Because their players were able to see visual evidence of their performance on an ongoing basis, their accuracy and execution improved.

While feedback was occurring throughout the engagements, sometimes coaches provided holistic feedback to the entire team during opening or closing team meetings at practice. Coach Rex shared:

> We have meetings at the end of each practice, we do a huddle -a light huddle before and a light huddle after and I also meet with my parent group immediately after practice. And I also, yeah, I'm old school, so I do give out little pieces of candies for those who do well during practice sessions.

Coach Rex explained that he and his coaches try and video his athletes at all the swim meets because this provides a tangible text for reference when the coach provides feedback to the swimmer. Although he acknowledged that he was not the best videographer, and laughed as he described his video footage as shaky with awkward camera angles because he was typically yelling encouragement for the swimmers. This was also observed at multiple swim meets as I often saw Coach Rex with his phone in one hand videoing a swimmer while yelling encouragement and waving his heat sheet around with his free hand.

Feedback, according to Coach Alex, could vary based on the swimmer and the situation. Sometimes, video was utilized, whereas, on other occasions, feedback was simply an oral conversation between the coach and the swimmer. Other times, coaches asked the swimmer to self-reflect on the race or their performance. However, he acknowledged that could sometimes be challenging due to the fact that some athletes were not as self-aware as others and could not always articulate their areas for improvement. In addition, personalities often played into this as well. Some swimmers were more aloof and were not as comfortable talking about their performance which posed a challenge. However, Coach Alex explained that feedback was a two-way street: "They have to be willing to listen to it and they also have to willing to digest what they are telling themselves (in their self-reflection) or what you're telling them." Coach Jason echoed this sentiment as he explained that providing the right type of feedback was a constant battle.

> I try not to give them feedback in a way that they don't want to receive it. But sometimes you have to be direct. When I start giving feedback, I try to get to know the person and develop a relationship with the swimmer first.

Coach Alex also acknowledged that, in some cases, more was not better. For some swimmers, he explained that providing feedback might happen on a less frequent basis. "Sometimes you just have to, you know, tell them once, remind them once, and then just kind of leave them alone for a while." Coach Alex recounted a specific swimmer where more feedback was not better and, in fact, it caused that athlete to overthink things, which slowed his progress and growth down significantly. Knowing each swimmer and what type of feedback to offer, along with the frequency, was key to getting results. In addition, Coach Alex explained that, in some cases, providing too much feedback too often created swimmers who were over-reliant on their coaches instead of shifting the responsibility onto themselves.

When discussing feedback, Coach Dan recounted an experience he had early on in his coaching.

> I did an internship at the University of Texas. I worked with the head coach, and he's been the head coach of five Olympic teams, and he's won more NCAA championships than any other swim coach in history. And he said a thing that he's got a goal; he's gonna talk to every swimmer at least five times during practice and for every negative thing he says, he's gonna say five positive things. So I've tried to incorporate that. And what I'll do is I will be walking around the deck and observing, looking for things that they're doing wrong most of all. And then focus on things that they're doing right and they things that they've improved on.

This experience guided Coach Dan's feedback cycle and principles as he attempted to follow this model in practice daily. While he had a set goal for positive reinforcement and criticism, as many of the other coaches explained regarding their athletes, Coach Dan's feedback varied based on the swimmer or the setting. He explained that, before a race, he attempted not to give athletes a lot of pre-race instructions that might overwhelm them and instead focused on a few focus items beforehand. Most of the pre-race instructions focused on technique or effort, with short and simple directives so that the athletes did not get overwhelmed or confused.

Sometimes, Coach Dan videoed the swimmers during their races and used the footage to provide feedback that incorporated video evidence which helped him draw attention to specific qualities of their race. He explained that he sometimes played the video with no sound so that the swimmer would pay attention to only what they saw instead of what they heard. As such, they were able to examine only the video footage and not the audio component. A lot of feedback consisted of Coach Dan getting input from the swimmers by simply asking them how they felt after the race. Offering the swimmers the opportunity to self-reflect helped them grow as swimmers and also begin to develop individual goals for their performance.

Each coach in this study indicated that understanding the needs of different athletes helped guide them in their methods of feedback delivery. No two athletes were treated exactly the same, and thus, feedback was unique and individualized. In addition, there was an apparent progression of feedback as the season evolved as many coaches encouraged their athletes to utilize self-reflection and peer-to-peer feedback. This variety of feedback allowed athletes to improve their performance throughout the season.

The beautiful thing about football is you cannot hide whether you know it or not. I can't cheat off of someone else's paper. Our overall goal is to win games.

—*Coach Wayne*

Planning for the next game or race often involved coaches and players developing a game plan or goal for achievement. Sometimes, these plans were team-centered, whereas, on other occasions, they were more individual for the athletes. However, in most cases, athletes were involved in the assessment and goal planning. In some instances, players wrote down their goals for the week as this helped them plan what they wanted to accomplish during that week of practice.

Sometimes these goals took on the form of simply improving their athleticism and performance by taking part in conditioning exercises. During the off-season, players cannot take part in official practice, but Coach Wayne worked on other aspects of training during this time. With their individual personal goals in mind, athletes developed training regimes with their coaches which helped them get bigger, faster, and stronger. Many athletes kept workout logs to track their progress, while others kept nutrition journals so that they could keep track of what they ate during these training phases. Keeping an accurate training journal helped the players determine whether or not they were meeting the goals they put in place for the season. In addition, Coach Wayne included a leader board in the weight room where players who lifted the most were displayed for the team to see (See Figure 5.1).

Coach Rex believed that goal setting was extremely important for his swimmers so he made certain that he tracked his swimmers' progress and helped them monitor and evaluate their goals.

Making sure they keep up with the heat sheets and things like that after swim meets is always a good way for kids to take a look at their own progression.

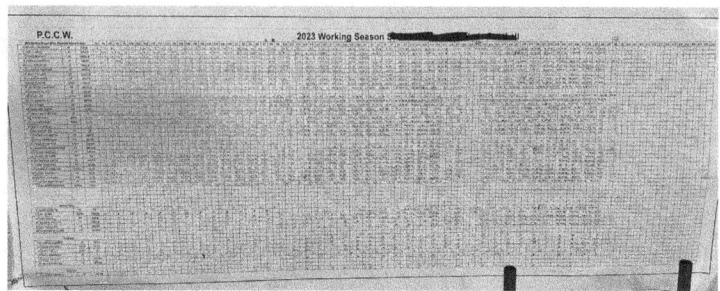

Figure 5.1 Workout Leaders List

But also to see whether or not they maximized their goals because with swimming, there are so many goals that they can achieve. The average kid swims about six races over the weekend (in a meet). If they're achieving one of their goals out of the six events or six races, then we're moving forward with what we're trying to do here.

By tracking their progress and communicating with his swimmers about their goals, Coach Rex helped to encourage individual accountability among his swimmers. When working with older swimmers, Coach Rex explained that goal setting was an even more important concept. This type of goal setting sometimes involved video recording practice, with swimmers reviewing the footage which was used for tracking their goals over the course of the season. This evidence and planning helped swimmers determine if they had met their goals for the season. In some ways, they were keeping a video journal that documented their progress throughout the season. In addition to this documentation, much of this involved a reflective component as swimmers were responsible for determining whether or not their performance was on track to make their goals or if they needed to make any adjustments.

For team sports, ultimately, the goal was winning the game or having a winning season as a team. As such, many of the goals were more team-centric, with the ultimate goal being that of a cohesive team. In individualized sports like swimming, many of the goals were centered on individual performances and beating their best times. However, regardless of the sport, coaches worked with their athletes to develop goals that would improve individualize performance and improve their physical, mental, and social well-being. To develop and execute these goals, coaches and players relied heavily on feedback that was presented frequently and through varied means. By focusing on the feedback portion of the instructional cycle, coaches were able to create, develop, and reinforce skills and concepts that athletes needed to be successful in their respective sports and meet their performance goals.

6 Overtime
Relationships Matter

> *How important are relationships? Very. Capital V. Capital E. Capital R. Capital Y. Very important.*
> —*Coach Ty*

As a university professor, I have encountered a number of faculty members and administrators in my career. One of the best deans I worked with told faculty on a regular basis, "People matter." Throughout the course of this study, I reflected back on Dr. K's mantra as it was evident that, for the coaches, their players mattered. Many explained that they could not accomplish their season or coaching goals without first and foremost building solid relationships with their athletes. They all acknowledged that this was not something that could be achieved overnight, but rather required prolonged time and effort on the part of the coach and athlete. Coaches in this study each had their own practices for building and fostering relationships, but relationships were a focus for all participants.

> *If someone comes into your house, what lengths would you go to protect your mama? We may not be mama, but we have to learn to fight for each other like that here. And the only way to do that is to respect and love each other here. And I think that takes you a really long way in your relationships.*
> —*Coach Wayne*

Relationships are one of the most important aspects of coaching, according to the participants in this study. Coach Wayne explained that he and his coaching staff worked hard to build a culture of genuine love, which he believed made his players play harder. That culture of love and respect was something that coaches relied on when their athletes needed criticism or tough love. Because they had built a culture based on the relationships they fostered with their athletes, some of this criticism and reflection came easier. As Coach Wes shared:

> You may see a coach getting on a kid hard and you might wonder why that kid comes back. We coach our kids hard, and we kind of let them understand

that life is hard. But these kids understand that every last one of these coaches cares about them. They (the players, aren't looking to run away, play somewhere else, or even quit. We can get on that kid on Monday, but he will be right back here on Tuesday. So the relationship is very important. A kid knows when you care about them.

Coach Wayne acknowledged that part of the reason that players perform for their coaches is due to the fact that they want to play the sport and enjoy the sport. "Football is something they want to do and they are willing to come to school to do it." Similarly, Coach Leon shared that many of his players came to school just to play football. They got their good grades because they wanted to play ball. As the head football coach, Coach Wayne explained that he often was approached by academic teachers who would sometimes complain about his players and their performance in their classes. Yet Coach Wayne wondered what type of relationships those teachers might have with his players. Is it a relationship with genuine care and concern or is it one where teachers are simply focused on grading and getting the work completed? However, Coach Neal explained that he was aware that in some cases part of the motivation for athlete performance came from their desire to get playing time. "We can carry it over their head with playing time. The biology teacher can't necessarily do that." In addition, many coaches worked to build a space for their athletes to share their opinions and ideas which helped with motivation. Coach Max explained:

> I got something they want, and they got a voice. I'm gonna listen to them. Is that what is happening in the classroom? I'm gonna be honest. You probably have some stupid ass seating chart. You gonna tell them when they can and cannot talk and when they can and cannot go to the trash can or sharpen their pencil. I'm not gonna do that. I mean, they might as well be incarcerated. I'm not gonna do that. I'm gonna listen to them and give them a voice. And not to throw it up in their faces, but ask the math teacher, "Do they call you and tell you happy birthday? Or happy anniversary or merry Christmas? Do you have kids that graduated fifteen years ago call you and tell you happy birthday every single time you have a birthday? I do." ... that comes from building a relationship. And because of that relationship they will run through a wall for me.

Although sometimes athletes were not as motivated in their academic classes, Coach Leon believed that having a good relationship with students could aid in improving motivation in the academic classroom as well. Because of the significant amount of time many players spent with their coaches, they held a level of trust and respect for coaches that they may not hold for another teacher. However, Coach Leon thought that if classroom teachers spent time getting to know their students better, they could determine what made each one "tick" and thus could improve the motivation and performance in the classroom.

Building these relationships was something that coaches had to work to achieve, and Coach Ty explained that building relationships started with studying people.

> You learn whoever you're coaching. You talk to them. And I think you have to be honest. You have to find out what makes that player go, what makes that player upset, what makes them happy. And you have to figure out how far you can go with them. Can you be rough with them? Can you talk to them any kind of way? There's a lot of stuff you have to figure out with that person and that comes from spending time with them. It comes from talking, observing, studying, and time.

Coach Tre also explained that building relationships with players did not involve only focusing on sports. Instead, coaches talked to their players about life, what music they liked, the foods they ate, their home situation, and more. Part of building those relationships involved getting to know the athlete as a whole person and not just a player on the team. In addition, Coach Neal acknowledged that many coaches were spending a significant amount of time with their players and often could work with them in smaller groups than in the classroom. This aided them in learning about their players not just as athletes, but as individuals.

While all the coaches in this study ultimately wanted their players to be successful in their sports, which often translated into winning, that was not the most important factor in their instruction. "Coaching goes beyond Xs and Os. You know, winning is important, but the relationships you build with these kids . . . you never forget it and the kids never forget it." Coach Todd went on to explain that while he certainly wanted to be successful on the field and score touchdowns, the greatest reward was when a player returned years later to tell a coach how much they meant to them. For these athletes, while their coaches often were hard on them and demanded peak physical performance and effort, the respect that they held for their coaching role models was significant. Part of this was attributed to the fact that many of the coaches in this study shared how their relationships helped them determine how to confront or address an issue with their athletes. As Coach Todd explained:

> You have to break them down sometimes to build them back up. But you have to know the kids. You might have one kid who can push through adversity when you stay on him 24/7, but then you have those kids who can't handle it. You have to be a very good observer and know these kids, so you know what makes them tick individually. That's where the relationships come in.

As Coach Todd explained, Coach Dean emphasized how important it was for coaches to be aware of their actions, how their words could be interpreted, and in turn, how this could impact their athletes. This was especially important when providing feedback. While Coach Alan shared that he often gave strong criticism to his swimmers, he believed that positivity was an important aspect of successful coaching. "You can be upset in the way somebody's doing something and you can tell them it's wrong, but you can do that with a positive attitude." Again, this came back to relationships.

Coach Wayne explained,

> People will play harder for you when you have a chance to build something special. And that's through the way we treat them. I hope they see that we care about them and that we love them. Relationships are the single most important thing.

In addition, coaches acknowledged that they were often asking their players to take part in activities that required them to go above and beyond their expectations and responsibilities as a student. Coach Hugh shared, "We're asking these student athletes to go to school for eight hours and then buy into what we're trying to sell. That doesn't happen without building a relationship."

Coach Cathy agreed as she explained that without building solid relationships with her athletes, she could not expect them to perform or accept criticism and feedback if her athletes didn't believe that their coach had their best interests at heart.

> I might make them mad, but they come back, and they might make me mad, but I come back. At the end of the day, I genuinely care about them, and they care about what they're doing and what we're trying to accomplish.

For these coaches, building relationships was just as important as building a game plan. Because each had goals they were chasing for success, making certain that they established a culture and environment that was built on trust and respect was a major component of their coaching instruction. Just like the fundamentals that they continued to work on throughout the season, relationship-building never stopped. It was a hallmark of the coaching programs in this study.

> *That's number one. If you don't trust me, we can't work together. And I think if I don't believe in your or your effort of energy, we can't work together.*
>
> —*Coach Max*

While relationships were the cornerstone of these athletic programs, developing and cultivating positive relationships took time and effort. For Coach

Alex, the most important aspect of coaching was trust. While he acknowledged that trust had to be built over time, he shared that in his experience, gaining trust occurred quicker with younger athletes. He equated this to the fact that many of the younger swimmers held an automatic respect for coaches, especially the senior or more advanced coaches. "Amelia has never ben coached by me, but she knew that I was the head coach and so there was this trust when she was 12, like, 'Oh, that's the senior coach.'" In some cases, like the one Coach Alex shared, athletes trusted the authority of the coach because of their track record and experience, which he believed gave them credibility. Yet even in those situations, trust was something that had to be earned and kept.

Similarly, Coach Dean believed everything went back to the word trust.

> They trust that you know what you're doing. That what you're telling them is right. They trust that you care about them. They gotta believe that you, what you're saying is the gospel and that on the field and off the field you actually care about them. They gotta trust that.

In addition, Coach Rex explained that the trust was not just between the athletes and their coaches, but it also extended to their parents and caregivers as well. Parents should trust their child's coach and believe that he/she is going to keep their kid safe, which directly affects whether or not a parent believes in a particular athletic program. "A kid will believe and trust and listen to a coach sometimes more than their parents because of the sport and that coach's connection to it." This was one of the reasons Coach Rex believed that parents needed to trust the coaches as well. When athletes see that their parents trust the coaches, they in turn are more likely to trust them as well.

Like other coaches shared, Coach Nate explained that trust was a major factor in relationships and coaching. However, that trust was a two-way street. "I think the coach has to trust that the athlete wants the best for themselves as well. And I think the athlete has to understand that the coach does want the best for them." This reciprocal relationship was not possible without the element of trust. While performance and execution certainly impact the results, building solid relationships with his players helped Coach Wayne and his coaching staff propel their players through rough spots and spur them on to a winning season. The relationships fostered between player and coach aided the staff in giving constructive feedback and providing the needed reinforcement for success and improved performance.

> *That's the thing a lot of people don't understand. I mean, we go get kids. We pick them up. I mean, I've had kids in my house. I've had kids that had to stay the night because something's going on at their house. The average person just doesn't understand that, or maybe doesn't realize it.*
> *—Coach Leon*

Like other coaches in this study, Coach Ty believed that many individuals who had never coached did not truly understand the amount of work and commitment that was involved. Sometimes, others were disgruntled about the stipends coaches received, but everyone in the study shared that they were not coaching for the money; they coached because they loved the sport and the athletes. In addition, when calculating the stipend amount by the number of hours coaches were logging, the extra pay really did not amount to much extra money.

Coach Ty shared that sometimes coaches were viewed differently in their schools because, on occasion, they did not have to attend after-school meetings or professional learning sessions. Yet coaches were often at school before classes began and were there long after the last bell rang. In addition, many coaches shared that they felt like they were evaluated differently and by a larger group of individuals as was explained by Coach Leon:

> In my experience, the math teacher isn't getting fired, you know 99% of the time. But there's 5,000 people out here every Friday night. The paper puts the score out there. The news puts the score out there. You know-you don't win, you're looking for a new job whether you're a great PE teacher or not. That's the nature. I think that is how it's different.

Coach Ty shared that not only was he evaluated by his administrator, but he was also evaluated by his players, fans, parents, and community members every time his players were on the court. And while Coach Cathy acknowledged that girls' basketball might be viewed differently than their male counterparts, she and her players were getting evaluated multiple times a week on their performance.

Aside from the difference in evaluation, Coach Dean shared that he believed coaches were viewed through a stereotypical lens.

> You know, people think all we do is hit people and talk loud and brag and score touchdowns and throw the ball down. You know, some people just think we show up on Friday nights and do stuff and win games.

In addition, Coach Hugh believed that those stereotypes continued into the classroom with coaches often being viewed as the teachers who showed movies all the time and didn't know how to teach. He went on to explain that, when he entered his graduate programs, he purposely did not disclose that he was a coach for fear of how his professors and colleagues might negatively view his intelligence and commitment.

While Coach Dan was not part of a public school system and thus did not have non-coaching colleagues, he did express that he felt as though his performance was evaluated by numerous individuals on a regular basis. This included his swimmers and parents of his athletes, but also other coaches and even other swimmers and parents not affiliated with his program as his coaching was on display at swim meets. In addition, Coach Dan explained that some observers might think that every season is executed in the same fashion and that coaching was something that was easy and didn't require a lot of effort.

> A lot of them think, "oh we just do the same thing as the year before." But that idea is assuming that was the best you could do. And what about things that have changed? And they're not looking at it as, you know, the kid is a year older-they need more challenges in that regard. So we always have to be evaluating, you know, what have we done in the past.

According to Coach Dan, no set stands alone, and his practice sets were always part of something bigger. Swim coaches, like other coaches in this study, log considerable hours on deck-often beginning with morning practices and ending with late evening practices to accommodate school schedules. In addition, when athletes had swim meets, these competitions often lasted for multiple consecutive days, with coaches on deck for sometimes over 12 hours a day. Thus, practice was never just an isolated practice. Instead, it was part of a bigger plan, with coaches planning and developing sets outside of practice time in addition to the time they logged on the pool deck.

Clearly, coaches in this study were logging countless hours, with many logging 14 or more hour days. When I asked Coach Neal if he thought people understood what was involved in coaching, he had this response:

> No, ma'am. I could tell you and that would be a whole 'nother book. You know, we go out there at the beginning of the year and it's going to be like 105 degrees and we're going to be out there for three hours and they're (colleagues) going to be upset because we missed a faculty meeting. They're going to be there (in the meeting) for thirty minutes, and you know, if they switched places with us would they go? So yeah, I wasn't there for the faculty meeting on a Tuesday, but I was here till midnight waiting on rides and doing laundry on Friday night and you were at home or at the bar with your friends.

Like his public-school coach colleagues, Coach Elliott explained that, for coaches, their coaching duties became like another full-time job. As almost all coaches had some type of teaching responsibility in schools, this made the number of hours they spent at school significantly higher than their colleagues.

Just as other coaches shared, Coach Alan does not believe that many people realize how much time and effort is involved in coaching. There is often a lot of pressure on coaches for their athletes to perform. Coach Alan recounted a time when some of his swimmers made it to the Olympic Trials. This achievement, while exciting, was also nerve-wracking and stressful for the coaches:

> Coaches don't get gold medals, but you know they're the ones who plan everything out and we coach and when something is not working, we have to adjust it, on the fly, in the middle. I don't think people think of swim coaches as that. Let's just say there's a lot of blood, sweat, and tears and anxiety for the kids to do well. I don't think they realize how much we want each individual kid to succeed.

In addition, coaches were often responsible for taking care of their players off the court and field. Many were frequently taking players to school or dropping them off at home after practice. When Coach Ty was head coach at another school, he shared that he never rode home by himself. He was always dropping a player off somewhere or taking them home if they missed the bus. And like Coach Wes shared:

> You have to understand, a lot goes on with a coach. Not just a football coach, but any coach. Period. You're a counselor, you're a father, you're a confidant, you're a religious leader. You have so many hats for these kids that you put on for these kids.

For the participants in this study, coaching was a multi-faceted job and one that required considerable commitment and dedication. Yet each one asserted how much they valued their roles as coaches because not only did they love their sports, but they also loved their athletes.

> *I don't like kids. I don't like hanging around kids. But I love swimmers. I'll bend over backwards for a swimmer. I'll go to the wall for a swimmer.*
> —Coach Alan

Part of the reason many coaches held such strong relationships with their athletes was due to the extended time spent with them. In some instances, coaches were spending well over 40 hours a week with a player which is significantly more than an Algebra teacher on a weekly basis. Coach Alan has worked with many of his athletes for multiple years and has watched them grow up.

> I've seen these kids more than their parents and I've been with them for X number of years and there is a relationship there. There's no doubt that when they are going out and the little baby birds leave the nest, it's really tough for me.

Coach Hugh believed that when polling students on their favorite teacher, when asked for the justification of their choice, most students would say that the teacher cared about them.

> Football coaches are the favorite teachers, and the reason why is there's that relationship. We drive them home. They don't have lunch money; they get lunch money from us. It's all that other stuff and maybe not all teachers signed up to be a teacher for that. Maybe they just like the content that they teach, and they believe that their content is important. But if you polled 100 students, 'Who's your favorite teacher and why?', the content is at the bottom of the list. It's all about the relationships—all of those interpersonal relationships. You know what it is? It's all that other stuff. And we get that because of the time we spend with them.

While coaching involved multiple aspects including foundational skills, structure, specific strategies, and feedback, all of those components were more effective and meaningful because of the personal relationships coaches developed with their athletes. While each coach had a different method and style, all asserted that unless they had an established bond of trust and a healthy relationship with their athletes, success was not possible. So while winning and success mattered, for the coaches in this study, people and relationships mattered most.

7 Next Season

What Can We Learn From Coaches?

> In a lot of schools, coaches are like heroes. You know, they command a certain type of respect. Very rarely am I called Mr., even by kids I don't coach. We get a lot of attention. I mean, even kids who don't play are asking me, 'Hey, Coach, y'all ready for the game? How'd you all do last night?' So that's another relationship.
>
> —Coach Cedric

A few years ago, when I was asked to conduct literacy professional learning sessions at a rural high school in Georgia, I never anticipated that I would spend most of my time in conversation with the athletic coaches about literacy and sports. These conversations made me contemplate how literacy is deeply ingrained in all we do, whether academic or not. My interactions with these athletic coaches spawned my interest in the intersection of sports and literacy, which resulted in a research project that carried me back to rural Georgia and South Carolina for more conversations and observations.

When I began this research over a year ago, I hoped that I would learn more about the literacy skills that coaches were employing in their coaching instruction mainly because I believed this would help educators, including myself, position literacy skills differently for our students. I hoped that I would learn more about any academic crossover that was occurring in athletics. However, I would be remiss if I did not share that a part of me was simply intrigued by the world of athletic coaching in general. As someone who has only experienced coaching from an adjacent perspective, I wanted to know more about what coaching practices looked like, but I really wanted to know how the academic skills, particularly literacy, were being taught and reinforced in a non-academic setting. As I know that many students do not see the direct connections between their academic worlds and personal ones, I thought that making an explicit connection between sports and academics could help bridge this gap between worlds.

After spending over a year interviewing coaches, observing practice and games, and examining documents, I began to understand the nature of athletic coaching and how it is connected to academic skills. While I began this study with a literacy lens, I also realized, through the progression of the study, that, in addition to the academic skills addressed, coaches were also employing a variety of feedback techniques, had developed extensive training plans and coaching structures, and relied heavily on the relationships they built with their athletes. In addition, the coaches possessed a complex level of knowledge that went beyond the rules of the game and proper technique, and they used this knowledge along with a number of instructional approaches to achieve their goals.

As a teacher educator, one of my main goals is to help teachers and students see the natural integration of reading and writing in daily life. My time in the field has given me even more examples of how much literacy infiltrates our daily lives. One of the coaches in this study, Coach Elliott, who is a personal friend of mine, has told me for years that I cannot make everything about literacy. Yet I believe I can, and I think he might be a little more convinced now after reading the findings in this study.

Aside from the fact that it is important to note that several literacy skills and practices were employed on a daily basis in the athletic setting, there is a lot that can be learned from coaches and their instructional practices that go beyond just the presence of literacy skills in their coaching. Transferring some of these practices into the classroom could be beneficial for all educators.

If you don't know their favorite colors and favorite foods and favorite song, don't cry when you're not successful.
—Coach Max

Throughout the course of this study, the importance of relationships continued to rise to the surface. Relationships were built over time, and this aided in the motivation of their players. While Coach Hugh believed that coaches had a unique gift for motivating their players, this motivation was a direct result of the relationships that coaches worked to build with their players.

> If teachers come watch this team practice, they're going to see how coaches interact with their athletes. They're gonna see upbeat; they're gonna see positive. They're gonna see a lot of reinforcements, but they're also gonna see hugs, they're gonna see high fives. They're gonna see all that stuff. There's a connection between the motivation and relationships.

In Coach Hugh's description of practice, he described the overall mood and culture of practice—one that is built on relationships with players along with positive feedback and reinforcement. In addition, as I observed practice across multiple sports, I noticed multiple opportunities where athletes interacted with their coaches. While the interactions might be brief, each player was addressed by a coach in some form of fashion, thus helping to facilitate a relationship through consistent and frequent communication.

For many coaches in this study, their relationships with their players continued long after they graduated or stopped playing the sport. In fact, Coach Cedric has jerseys displayed in his classroom from his former players who went on to play in college. As many of his players continued their basketball careers in college, he requested they bring him one of their college jerseys to hang in his room for all his students to see. During my interview with Coach Cedric, I was in awe of the number of college jerseys he has collected over the years and this visual display of his coaching impact. He told me about each player as he went jersey by jersey telling me about each of his former players.

Many of the coaches shared that one of the most rewarding aspects of coaching was watching their athletes grow up and see how they evolved into adults. Often players connected with their coaches long after they left with many reaching out to tell their coaches how grateful they were for the lessons they learned while they were playing with them. In addition, many coaches tried to attend the games and races of their former athletes even after they moved on from their programs. For academic teachers, building strong relationships in the classroom, like those described by the coaches in this study, could have an impact on student performance and motivation. Coaches in this study suggested that classroom teachers take an interest in their students' outside activities, attend games when possible, and ask them about their games even when they cannot attend. These small gestures could help teachers in building relationships not only with their student-athletes but also with their other students. From a personal perspective, when I was a middle grades teacher, I made a point to ask my athletes about their games and I often sent articles about the players to them in the mail. A few years ago, I ran into a former student-athlete at the local I-Hop. Guess what he remembered about my class? Not the writing I taught, but the fact that I used to mail him newspaper clippings of his basketball and football games whenever he was listed in the paper. Think about that for a minute: It was not the content he remembered, but rather the relationship.

While Coach Wes recognized that some of his players would perform for him on the field but would not necessarily produce in the classroom, he did believe that by taking an interest in students and developing engaging lessons, athletes may perform better in the classroom. "You have to try and make it fun and enjoyable for them. Try to find a way to relate to something they like." While he acknowledged that motivating athletes was sometimes easier, the reward being that, when they performed, they got more play time and scored points, he believed that this type of motivation could transfer in the classroom. It was a matter of connecting with students and making them see how they could benefit from what they were learning. In addition, as Coach Todd shared, many of the athletes were coming in early and staying late for practice, but the first period did not stop them. They were expected to come in and perform like any other student who had not been at school for extra time. Recognizing the commitment and hard work of their student-athletes might help teachers understand them on a different level.

For classroom teachers, taking a page from the coach's playbook on relationships could have significant impacts in classrooms. As all coaches in this study shared that they were responsible for offering constructive criticism to their players, having a relationship with their athletes assisted them when they needed to have these types of conversations. In addition, coaches studied their athletes and used their observations to determine how to interact with their players. Without this working knowledge of their athletes, their communications might be misinterpreted or could be ineffective. As Coach Jason explained, for coaches to be successful, they needed to have a strong command for communication as this was important for clarity and buy-in from athletes. This was echoed by Coach Wes who shared that everything coaches and players do comes down to communication, which was one of the reasons why coaches relied on multiple modalities when presenting a skill or delivering feedback. No coach in this study delivered material using only one modality; instead, each determined how to best present information to their athletes based on the needs and characteristics of each individual. This was only possible through the cultivation and nurturing of strong relationships.

For educators, spending time getting to know their students could provide significant benefits in the classroom. As Coach Cathy shared, "Before I can go make it happen with this group of kids, before I can teach you math or I can teach you anything, I have to know who you are." Through building relationships and paying attention to individual needs, teachers can plan instruction that builds on this knowledge which could yield success in the classroom. Building relationships with students can help teachers identify what literature to suggest, how to approach a math problem, or what materials to bring in when addressing a specific standard or skill. This can translate into increased motivation and performance in the academic classroom.

I mean it is constant. They are always getting feedback. On film, in writing, in person, on the field, whole team, small group-you name it. Feedback is constant.

—**Coach Elliott**

In the coaching setting, feedback to the athletes was something that was occurring on a frequent basis through a variety of modalities. While there was sometimes a small delay between an athlete's performance or action and feedback delivery, this delay was abbreviated. In most cases, feedback was instantaneous, with athletes getting verbal or visual cues on their performance.

For example, at a recent swim meet, I watched multiple swimmers climb out of the pool and go straight to their coaches for feedback after their races. In some instances, swimmers were given corrective comments that they would use in future races, and in other instances, they were given positive feedback based on some aspect of their performance. In fact, for some swimmers, their feedback was a fist pound or a high five. It was all dependent on the swimmer and the race, along with the amount of time the coach had for discussion. Sometimes, coaches had multiple athletes in a group providing overall feedback, while on other occasions, they discussed race performance individually with the swimmer. While the feedback that was provided differed based on the swimmer, the immediacy did not. This was especially important as this immediate feedback allowed athletes to correct errors on the spot and improve their overall meet performance.

When thinking about this method of feedback for the classroom, having opportunities to provide feedback often and through a variety of approaches can help students improve their academic performance. Instead of waiting until the summative assessment, offering opportunities for formative assessment throughout a unit or at different times during the week can give students valuable information on their performance. In addition, by incorporating assessments along the way, teachers can determine which areas might need additional focus or supplemental instruction and which components or skills have already been mastered. While these ongoing assessments are certainly beneficial for the students, they are also valuable for teachers. Data from ongoing assessments can help drive instruction and allow teachers to design engagements that capitalize on student competencies while also addressing any areas for growth.

Perhaps another tip educators might take from coaches is the method by which feedback is delivered and how that feedback will be used to achieve specific goals. In many instances, students receive feedback through one modality and that often is in written form. As I observed the coaches in this study, I noticed that in almost all instances coaches utilized a layered approach when delivering feedback. For example, coaches often gave oral feedback while sketching out diagrams of plays or showing videos of race or game performance simultaneously (See Figure 7.1). In addition, coaches shifted from whole group feedback to individual feedback seamlessly and often. When thinking about how this might translate into the classroom, teachers might consider layering their feedback approaches as well, along with varying how they deliver feedback. For example, utilizing diagrams, video clips, and images along with traditional written feedback could help some students improve their performance. In addition, coaches worked with their athletes to use the feedback they provided to develop goals for the season, next race, or next game. Thus, athletes were using that feedback to help plan and achieve their individual and team goals. In some instances in the classroom, students might be given feedback, but they could be uncertain about what to do with it. Helping students first develop instructional goals and then use any feedback to help them meet their set goals can help students recognize the value of feedback and how it can assist them in their end games.

> *I think you got to be transparent with the program. I think you got to invite people over. Show up and come see what we do. You know, the transparency and letting people publicly see your program and what you do every day. I think that goes a long way.*
>
> —*Coach Leon*

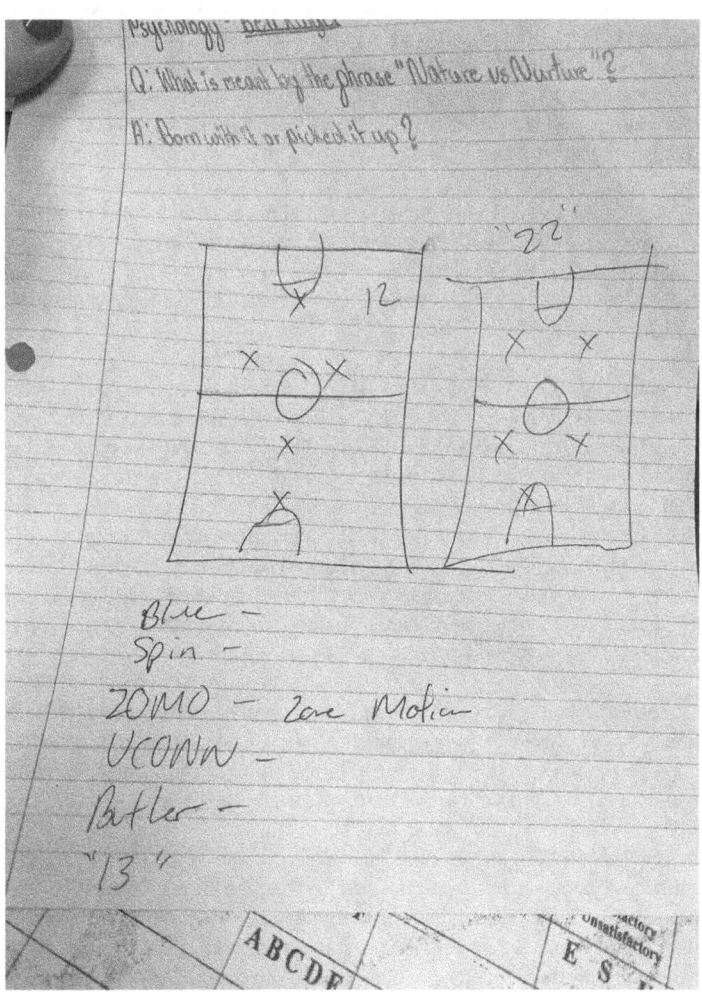

Figure 7.1 Basketball Diagram

Coaches in this study indicated that they welcomed their colleagues to get involved in their work and would be willing to share their insights and approaches. Many coaches shared that they already worked collaboratively with their colleagues to help ensure that their players would be successful. While athletics was certainly important, several shared that making certain their players were academically successful was equally important which often involved communication and cooperation between teachers and coaches. Coach Leon shared that like teachers, coaches did not get to pick their athletes. While collegiate and professional coaches were able to recruit their players, youth coaches had to work with what they were given, just like classroom teachers. Building opportunities for communication and collaboration between coaches and other educators could offer numerous benefits. Coach Todd emphasized the importance of these collaborations between coaches, teachers, and support staff.

> I dealt hand in hand with our instructional coaches to make sure our kids were getting their SAT prep and ACT prep. And the players worked hard with me hand in hand. They did before school. They did after school and did whatever it takes. Everybody wins when the kid gets to the podium and signs a scholarship. We all win.

Coach Todd's explanation of collaboration between coaches and teachers is one that has an end goal of student success and academic achievement in mind. However, many school-based coaches shared that teachers typically only reached out to coaches for assistance when one of their players was not performing academically. In many of those contacts, teachers wanted the coach to do something to "make" the athlete perform and often approached the coach as the problem solver instead of as one who would partner in the student's success. Yet every coach in this study shared that they welcomed opportunities to work with teachers and athletes to make the student successful. During one observation, Coach Wayne told his players:

> Y'all have exams tomorrow. Make sure you are here. We can't overcome a zero 'cause it's 20% of your grade. You need a ride, holler and we'll come get you. It ain't no problem. Finish. Finish strong. Bring all your textbooks and notes and stuff with you. Come see me and we'll study.

For coaches, success meant more than just winning on the field or court or achieving a personal best time; instead, it was part of a collaborative commitment to success, both on and off the field. The best way for them to make this success happen was to provide coaching instruction that was effective, but also work with their athletes for their academic success. For this to be effective, working with their colleagues was imperative. In addition, Coach Leon explained that many of their tactics were ones that had been refined over time. Rarely did coaches do a complete shift and totally overhaul their coaching plans.

> I think coaches do a good job of adjusting and not wholesale scrapping everything. Like I feel we do a bad job in education. I would never change behavior management systems every two years. We don't do that in the coaching field. While we might make small adjustments and changes, we don't scrap the whole thing and completely change everything.

With this in mind, teachers might begin to deliberately involve their coaching colleagues in their instructional goals and classroom demands, which could be achieved through conversations and communication. In this study, each coach shared the openness and willingness to share their goals and methods in their sports coaching. Because some coaches believed that those who did not coach might not understand the commitment and dedication many athletes put into their sports, they expressed their desire for educators to come to watch practice so they might better understand what was going on with their athletic programs. Building a successful collaborative community in schools and community sports means including stakeholders across disciplines to better serve students.

> *I tell everybody. You will get fired faster for being a bad coach than for being a bad teacher. Every coach in the world knows that.*
> —Coach Wes

While all the coaches in this study believed that people outside of coaching did not always understand how much time and effort went into coaching, those in the school setting shared their perceptions on attitudes toward coaches. Many explained how they were evaluated not only by their administrators for their teaching performance and overall job duties but also by the community and fans. As Coach Neal shared, "Not to sound ugly right now, but 5,000 people don't turn out to watch the biology test."

Coach Max echoed the scrutiny that many coaches were under as the community and fans expected coaches to perform by winning.

> They gonna fire you. You pay $10 for a ticket and watch my ass get beat by fifty points the next two Friday nights and somebody's gonna put a damn "for sale" sign in my yard.

Winning and performing well were at the forefront of each coach's season plan as they were aware that their performance as a coach was being evaluated constantly. Coach Cathy shared that, in addition to the evaluations she received from her administrator on her classroom instruction, her evaluations continued on the court. "I get evaluated every Tuesday, Friday, and Saturday." Like other coaches shared, they found their performance and effectiveness were evaluated by a large constituency which often included individuals who might only see what occurred on game night and not all the planning and training that occurred before. A loss of a game or a poor race performance is only a snapshot of a program or an athlete's performance. Similarly, in the classroom when a student does not perform well on an assessment, a failing test grade only gives a snapshot of performance and does not consider the planning, practice, and instruction the students received prior. That one assessment does not take into account a student's absentee record, home experiences, overall health, or other outside factors that might affect performance. One performance should not be an indicator of success or failure, but rather a data point in a comprehensive program that measures the overall growth and performance of an individual.

I think I've gotten as much or more from the sport as a coach than I did as an athlete.

—**Coach Nate**

It was clear from the interviews and observations that the coaches in this study had a passion for their sport. Each genuinely enjoyed being there, and while Coach Nate shared that everyone had days where they might not want to be at work, having a passion for the sport you are coaching was necessary as the athletes were able to pick up on who wanted to be on deck or at practice and who did not. Having a coach who is excited about the sport and has a passion for coaching could help when times might get difficult or when athletes hit a rough spot in the season. In addition, coaches in this study showed a strong commitment and dedication to their programs and athletes. This was evident as they described the hours they logged coaching, planning, and taking care of items that might not be coaching related such as athlete transportation, food, and money for athletic supplies. For many, it was all about the coaching and their athletes. Just recently I ran into Coach Rex at a swim meet and noticed he had traded in his signature cornrow braids for a short haircut. When I asked him about the change, he smiled and remarked:

> I'm getting in the water more with the kids so I can teach the development group and my braids were a mess. So I got it cut. It's easier and I can get in the water with the kids and teach.

This brief conversation with Coach Rex reminded me again of how sports and athlete-centric these coaches' lives were.

Like the coaches in this study, having classroom teachers who share their passion for their content and exhibit this excitement can have positive impacts on instruction and performance. Exhibiting genuine excitement for the content that is taught, but, most importantly, demonstrating genuine care and concern for those individuals in the classroom can yield a number of benefits.

Overall, there is much that can be learned from athletic coaches, not just in their literacy engagements but overall. Not only are athletics coaches teaching and reinforcing academic skills such as inferencing, using textual evidence, and completing close reads, but they are also teaching youth how to utilize and respond to feedback and plan, develop, and achieve their goals. Taking athletics coaches as active partners in education and utilizing some of their tactics and approaches can help educators build instructional experiences that are effective, meaningful, and engaging.

References

Bennett, T. (2017). *Creating a culture: How school leaders can optimize behavior*. Department for Education.

Blomfield, C. J., & Barber, B. L. (2011). Developmental experiences during extracurricular activities and Australian adolescents' self-concept: Particularly important for youth from disadvantaged schools. *Journal of Youth and Adolescence, 40*(5), 582–594. https://doi.org/10.1007/s10964-010-9563-0

Bowker, A., Gadbois, S., & Cornock, B. (2003). Sports participation and self-esteem: Variations as a function of gender and gender role orientation. *Sex Roles, 49*, 47–58. https://doi.org/10.1023/A:1023909619409

Burns, R. D., Brusseau, T. A., Fu, Y., Myrer, R. S., & Hannon, J. C. (2016). Comprehensive school physical activity programming and classroom behavior. *American Journal of Health Behavior, 40*(1), 100–107. https://doi.org/10.5993/AJHB.40.1.11

Burns, R. D., Fu, Y., Brusseau, T. A., Clements-Nolle, K., & Yang, W. (2018). Relationships among physical activity, sleep duration, diet, and academic achievement in a sample of adolescents. *Preventive Medicine Reports, 12*, 71–74. https://doi.org/10.1016/j.pmedr.2018.08.014

Clark, H. J., Camiré, M., Wade, T. J., & Cairney, J. (2015). Sport participation and its association with social and psychological factors known to predict substance use and abuse among youth: A scoping review of the literature. *International Review of Sport and Exercise Psychology, 8*(1), 224–250. https://doi.org/10.1080/1750984X.2015.1068829

Donnelly, J. E., Hillman, C. H., Castelli, D., Etnier, J. L., Lee, S., Tomporowski, P., Lambourne, K., & Szabo-Reed, A. N. (2016). Physical activity, fitness, cognitive function, and academic achievement in children: A systematic review. *Medicine and Science in Sports and Exercise, 48*(6), 1197–1222. https://doi.org/10.1249/MSS.0000000000000901

Eime, R. M., Young, J. A., Harvey, J. T., Charity, M. J., & Payne, W. R. (2013). A systematic review of the psychological and social benefits of participation in sport for children and adolescents: Informing development of a conceptual model of health through sport. *The International Journal of Behavioral Nutrition and Physical Activity, 10*, 98. https://doi.org/10.1186/1479-5868-10-98

References

Fredricks, J. A., & Eccles, J. S. (2006). Is extracurricular participation associated with beneficial outcomes? Concurrent and longitudinal relations. *Developmental Psychology, 42*(4), 698–713. https://doi.org/10.1037/0012-1649.42.4.698

Freire, P. (2000). *Pedagogy of the oppressed* (30th anniversary). Continuum.

Freire, P., & Macedo, D. (1987). *Literacy: Reading the word and the world* (1st ed.). Routledge. https://doi.org/10.4324/9780203986103

Harper, R. (2014). Making sense of texts. *SRATE Journal, 23*(2), 21–27.

Harper, R. (2017). *Content writing that rocks (and works!)*. Shell Education.

Hattie, J., & Timperley, H. (2007). The power of feedback. *Review of Educational Research, 77*(1), 81–112. https://doi.org/10.3102/003465430298487

Hattie, J., & Zierer, K. (2019). *Visible learning insights*. Routledge, an Imprint of the Taylor & Francis Group.

Hillman, C. H., Erickson, K. I., & Hatfield, B. D. (2017). Run for your life! Childhood physical activity effects on brain and cognition. *Kinesiology Review, 6*(1), 12–21. https://doi.org/10.1123/kr.2016-0034

Kort-Butler, L. A. (2012). Extracurricular activity involvement and adolescent self-esteem. *PsycEXTRA Dataset*. https://doi.org/10.1037/e535002013-004

Kort-Butler, L. A., & Hagewen, K. J. (2011). School-based extracurricular activity involvement and adolescent self-esteem: A growth-curve analysis. *Journal of Youth and Adolescence, 40*(5), 568–581. https://doi.org/10.1007/s10964-010-9551-4

Marzano, R. J., & Marzano, J. S. (2003). The key to classroom management. *Educational Leadership, 61*(1), 6–13.

Peirce, C. (1955). Logic as semiotic: The theory of signs. In J. Buchler (Ed.), *Philosophical writings of peirce* (pp. 98–128). Dover Publications Inc.

Sadler, D. R. (2010). Beyond feedback: Developing student capability in complex appraisal. *Assessment & Evaluation in Higher Education, 35*, 535–550. https://doi.org/10.1080/02602930903541015

Taylor, M., & Turek, G. (2010). If only she would play? The impact of sports participation on self-esteem, school adjustment, and substance abuse among rural and urban African American girls. *Journal of Sport Behavior, 33*(3), 315–336.

Te Velde, S. J., Lankhorst, K., Zwinkels, M., Verschuren, O., Takken, T., de Groot, J., & Hays Study Group. (2018). Associations of sport participation with self-perception, exercise self-efficacy and quality of life among children and adolescents with a physical disability or chronic disease-a cross-sectional study. *Sports Medicine—Open, 4*(1), 38. https://doi.org/10.1186/s40798-018-0152-1

Tovani, C. (2000). *I read it, but I don't get it: Comprehension strategies for adolescent readers*. Stenhouse Publishers.

Whitley, M., Massey, W., & Wilkison, M. (2018). A systems theory of development through sport for traumatized and disadvantaged youth. *Psychology of Sport and Exercise, 38*, 116–125. https://doi.org/10.1016/j.psychsport.2018.06.004

Wright, J. (2014). Participation in the classroom: Classification and assessment techniques. *Teaching Innovation Projects*, *4*, 1–11.

Zwinkels, M., Verschuren, O., Balemans, A., Lankhorst, K., te Velde, S., van Gaalen, L., de Groot, J., Visser-Meily, A., & Takken, T. (2018). Effects of a school-based sports program on physical fitness, physical activity, and Cardiometabolic Health in youth with physical disabilities: Data from the sport-2-stay-fit study. *Frontiers in Pediatrics*, *6*. https://doi.org/10.3389/fped.2018.00075

Index

academic skills 22, 43, 93
assessments 71, 79, 81, 96, 100

basketball 12–14, 19, 23, 27, 32, 35, 60, 73

Coach Aaron 12, 18, 60, 75, 76, 77
Coach Adam 12, 28
Coach Alan 12, 17, 73–74, 86, 89, 90
Coach Alex 12, 42, 48, 49, 55, 64, 79, 80, 82, 87
Coach Cathy 12, 27, 28, 31, 40–41, 46, 61, 62, 75–76, 86, 95, 100
Coach Cedric 12, 18, 26, 44, 45, 63, 64, 92
Coach Dan 12, 16–18, 38, 46, 49, 64, 74, 80
Coach Dean 12, 16, 31, 32, 40, 48, 56, 58, 60, 63, 69, 73, 86–89
Coach Elliot 13, 21, 38–39, 48, 51, 64, 67–69, 72, 89, 93, 95
Coach Gary 13, 18, 40, 41, 46–47, 49, 50–51, 60, 65–66, 74, 77
Coach Hugh 13, 21, 23, 40–41, 43, 61, 63, 73, 78, 86, 88, 91, 99
Coach Jason 13, 17, 79, 82, 95
Coach Leon 13, 29, 30, 33, 37, 47, 48, 56–57, 75, 84, 87–88, 98–99
Coach Max 13, 21, 25, 30, 38, 40, 49, 67, 75, 86, 93, 99
Coach Nate 13, 17, 18, 22, 87, 100
Coach Neal 13, 16, 21, 33, 40, 41, 63, 84–85, 89, 99
Coach Rex 13, 17, 42, 55, 79, 81, 82, 87, 100
Coach Tim 13, 39, 48
Coach Todd 13, 21, 32, 36, 38, 52, 56, 59, 62, 68, 72–73, 77, 85, 94, 98
Coach Ty 13, 18, 19, 20, 25, 27, 31, 33, 35, 39, 40, 73, 83
Coach Wayne 14–16, 23–27, 29, 35, 38, 74, 77–78, 81, 83–84, 86, 87, 98
Coach Wes 14, 35, 45, 47, 50, 58, 63, 72, 74–75, 90, 94–95, 99

feedback 8, 34, 50, 71–82, 93, 95–97
film 31–32, 34, 45, 47
football 6, 12–14, 21, 24, 26–27, 32, 35, 43, 48, 52, 55, 59, 61, 63, 66, 69–70, 77, 84, 91
foundational/fundamental skills 15, 18, 19–23, 25, 26, 28–30, 37, 48, 91

gymnastics 6

karate 4

language 52–53, 58, 65
literacy 4, 8, 11, 12, 29, 36, 45, 51, 92, 101
literacy engagements 1–2, 22, 23, 26

narratives 36

performance 18, 25, 30, 32–34, 45, 48, 78, 79, 82, 84–88, 96, 99, 100, 101
philosophy 42
players- 2 15, 16–19, 23–24, 27–35, 38, 42–43, 45, 52, 56, 60, 62–63, 75, 84
practice 15–19, 21–23, 32–33, 36, 51, 61, 74, 80, 89

schedule/routine 15–16, 22
skills (academic and athletes) 28–30, 38, 40–42, 44, 47, 65
strategies for learning 33, 37
structure 15, 17, 21

swimming 4, 12–13, 17–18, 25, 28, 32, 38, 41, 42

writing strategies 8

For Product Safety Concerns and Information please contact our EU
representative GPSR@taylorandfrancis.com
Taylor & Francis Verlag GmbH, Kaufingerstraße 24, 80331 München, Germany

www.ingramcontent.com/pod-product-compliance
Lightning Source LLC
Chambersburg PA
CBHW051756230426
43670CB00012B/2313